Great Meals in Minutes was created by
Rebus, Inc.
and published by Time-Life Books.

Rebus, Inc.
Publisher: Rodney Friedman
Editor: Shirley Tomkievicz
Executive Editor: Elizabeth P. Rice
Art Director: Ronald Gross
Managing Editor: Brenda Goldberg
Senior Editor: Cara De Silva
Food Editor and Food Stylist: Grace Young
Photographer: Steven Mays
Prop Stylist: Cathryn Schwing
Staff Writer: Alexandra Greeley
Associate Editor: Jordan Verner
Editorial Assistants: Bonnie J. Slotnick,
Joan Michel
Assistant Food Stylist: Nancy Leland
Thompson
Recipe Tester: Gina Palombi Barclay

For information about any Time-Life book,
please write:
Reader Information
Time-Life Books
541 North Fairbanks Court
Chicago, Illinois 60611

Library of Congress Cataloging in Publication Data
Fish & shellfish menus.
    (Great meals in minutes)
    Includes index.
    1. Cookery (Fish)   2. Cookery (Shellfish)
3.Menus.   4. Cooks—United States—Biography.
I. Time-Life Books.   II. Title: Fish and shellfish
menus.   III. Series.
TX747.F4938   1984   641.6′92   84-2567
ISBN 0-86706-179-0 (lib. bdg.)
ISBN 0-86706-178-2 (retail ed.)

Time-Life Books Inc.
is a wholly owned subsidiary of
Time Incorporated
Founder: Henry R. Luce 1898–1967
Editor-in-Chief: Henry Anatole Grunwald
President: J. Richard Munro
Chairman of the Board: Ralph P. Davidson
Corporate Editor: Jason McManus
Group Vice President, Books: Joan D. Manley

Time-Life Books Inc.
Editor: George Constable
Executive Editor: George Daniels
Director of Design: Louis Klein
Board of Editors: Dale M. Brown, Thomas
A. Lewis, Robert G. Mason, Ellen Phillips,
Peter Pocock, Gerry Schremp, Gerald
Simons, Rosalind Stubenberg, Kit van
Tulleken, Henry Woodhead
Director of Administration: David L. Harrison
Director of Research: Carolyn L. Sackett
Director of Photography: John Conrad Weiser

President: Reginald K. Brack Jr.
Senior Vice President: William Henry
Vice Presidents: George Artandi, Stephen L.
Bair, Robert A. Ellis, Juanita T. James,
Christopher T. Linen, James L. Mercer,
Joanne A. Pello, Paul R. Stewart

Editorial Operations
Design: Anne B. Landry (art coordinator);
James J. Cox (quality control)
Research: Phyllis K. Wise (assistant director),
Louise D. Forstall
Copy Room: Diane Ullius
Production: Celia Beattie, Gordon E. Buck,
Correspondent: Miriam Hsia (New York)

SERIES CONSULTANT
Margaret E. Happel is the author of *Ladies
Home Journal Adventures in Cooking,
Ladies Home Journal Handbook of Holiday
Cuisine,* and other best-selling cookbooks, as
well as the translator and adapter of Rebecca
Hsu Hiu Min's *Delights of Chinese Cooking.*
A food consultant based in New York City,
she has been director of the food department
of *Good Housekeeping* and editor of
American Home magazine.

WINE CONSULTANT
Tom Maresca combines a full-time career
teaching English literature with writing
about and consuming fine wines. He is now
at work on *The Wine Case Book,* which
explains the techniques of wine tasting.

Cover: Kathleen Sanderson's seafood soup
Provençale with chèvre florentine and garlic
bread. See pages 70–71.

Great Meals
IN MINUTES

FISH & SHELLFISH
MENUS

TIME-LIFE BOOKS, ALEXANDRIA, VIRGINIA

Contents

MEET THE COOKS 4

FISH AND SHELLFISH IN MINUTES 7

EQUIPMENT 15

PANTRY 16

LESLIE LAND 18

Steamed Lobster with Four Sauces
Sautéed New Cabbage / Oven-Fried Potatoes 20

Broiled Shark Steaks with Lime-Parsley Sauce
Rice with Walnuts / Broiled Vegetables 22

Lemon-Braised Celery, Endive, and Watercress
Haddock with Crab Meat and Hazelnut Stuffing 25

PAUL NEUMAN AND STACY BOGDONOFF 28

Poached Salmon with Green Sauce
Rice Pilaf with Scallions / Asparagus with Lemon Glaze 30

Mediterranean Fish Stew / Basil Toasts
Watercress and Endive Salad with Warm Olive Oil Dressing 32

Broiled Swordfish with Herb Butter / Sautéed Spinach with Shallots
New Potatoes Braised in Broth with Leeks 35

PATRICIA UNTERMAN 38

Avocado and Grapefruit Salad with Walnut Oil Dressing
Creole Fish and Oyster Stew / Baked Rice with Almonds 40

Fish Baked in Parchment with Red Peppers
Polenta with Butter and Cheese / Marinated Salad 42

Fresh Tomato and Fennel Soup / Trout Baked in Coarse Salt
Chard in Butter and Garlic / New Potatoes with Basil 45

JOSEPHINE ARALDO 48

Quenelles with Shallot Sauce
Potatoes with Onions and Cheese / Sautéed Carrots and Grapes 50

Avocado and Potato Soup
Fillets of Sole in Wine Sauce / Zucchini Merveille 52

Lima Bean Soup
Whiting with Lemon Sauce / Cucumbers and Brussels Sprouts 55

BRUCE CLIBORNE 58

Sautéed Scallops with White Wine / Spicy Spinach Sauté
Wild Mushroom Salad with Basil and Mint 60

Mussels and Shrimp in Coconut Cream with Mint
Stuffed Kohlrabi 62

Clams in Sesame-Ginger Sauce
Fettuccine with Garlic and Oil / Mixed Vegetables, Oriental Style 66

KATHLEEN KENNY SANDERSON 68

Seafood Soup Provençale
Chèvre Florentine / Garlic Bread 70

Rainbow Trout / Julienned Vegetables
Saffron Rice Mold 72

Sea Bass with Fennel-Butter Sauce
Warm Potato Salad / Garden Salad with Mustard Vinaigrette 74

MARK MILLER 78

Spicy Squid Salad / Broiled Tuna with Orange-Cumin Sauce
Sauté of Squash, Onions, and Peppers 80

Oyster Seviche
Baked Red Snapper with Chili Sauce / Green Rice 82

Salmon à la Tartare
Poached Oysters with Saffron-Cream Sauce 84

ELISABETH THORSTENSSON 86

Fillets of Sole in Herb Butter / Riced Potatoes with Parsley
Sautéed Snow Peas with Water Chestnuts 88

Seafood Curry Chowder
Bibb Lettuce, Avocado, and Tomato Salad 90

Chicken Liver Mousse
Fillets of Brook Trout with Mushroom Sauce / Spicy Rice 92

LINDA JOHNSON 94

Prawns with Green Peppercorns / Snow Peas and Jícama
Orzo with Poppy Seeds 96

Steamed Mussels / Brown Rice with Roasted Red Pepper
Asparagus Vinaigrette with Pecans 98

Bourbon-Basted Salmon
Bulgur Pilaf / Spinach and Kiwi Salad 101

ACKNOWLEDGMENTS 103 INDEX 103

Meet the Cooks

LESLIE LAND

Food writer and food consultant Leslie Land, who now lives on the Maine coast, was raised on a farm in the Pennsylvania Dutch country. She began her cooking career during college when she worked as a part-time caterer. After college, she cooked at Chez Panisse restaurant in California. She writes a syndicated weekly food column, and contributes articles to *Yankee*, *Food & Wine*, and *Cuisine*. She is an activist on soil conservation and world agricultural problems.

PAUL NEUMAN AND STACY BOGDONOFF

Stacy Bogdonoff and her husband Paul Neuman are native New Yorkers. Stacy Bogdonoff graduated from the Culinary Institute of America, then attended advanced classes at L'Ecole de Cuisine La Varenne in Paris. Paul Neuman apprenticed with a private caterer and has taught a class in fish and seafood cookery at the New York Restaurant School. Together they own, operate, and cook for Neuman & Bogdonoff, a Manhattan retail food store and catering service in New York City.

PATRICIA UNTERMAN

Patricia Unterman studied cooking with Josephine Araldo, a Cordon Bleu-trained chef and a contributor to this volume. As co-owner of the Hayes Street Grill in San Francisco, which specializes in fresh seafood, she creates new fish recipes daily, experimenting with uncommon varieties of seafood. She is also the restaurant critic for the *San Francisco Chronicle*.

JOSEPHINE ARALDO

Josephine Araldo was born in Brittany at the turn of the century. She attended Le Cordon Bleu for four and a half years and cooked professionally in Paris for such clients as dancer Isadora Duncan. Since the early 1920s, she has lived in Northern California, working first as a private cook, then conducting cooking courses, and later preparing meals for the Catholic fathers of Notre Dame des Victoires. She is the author of *Cooking with Josephine* and *Sounds from Josephine's Kitchen*.

BRUCE CLIBORNE

Chef, food stylist, recipe developer, and caterer Bruce Cliborne experiments with elements of every kind of cuisine. A native Virginian, he moved to New York, and began to work in restaurants; he has now been dinner chef at the Soho Charcuterie for several years and has taught at the New York Restaurant School and the New School for Social Research. Bruce Cliborne was a contributing author of and food stylist for the *Soho Charcuterie Cookbook*.

KATHLEEN KENNY SANDERSON

Kathleen Kenny Sanderson, who lives in New York, is a graduate of the California Culinary Academy in San Francisco. She cooked at L'Escargot in San Francisco, and later was personal chef for the Robert Kennedy family. Besides teaching cooking at the New School for Social Research, she is the Food Editor and Test Kitchen Director at *Restaurant Business* magazine. She received the Jesse H. Neal Certificate of Merit for her monthly Menu Ideas section of the magazine.

MARK MILLER

Born and raised in Boston, Mark Miller now lives in Berkeley. A former graduate student in anthropology, he has a scholar's approach to cooking and has studied with several chefs. He began to cook as chef at Chez Panisse in Berkeley, where he worked from 1975 to 1979. He opened both the Fourth Street Grill and the Santa Fe Bar and Grill in Berkeley. Now, he is sole owner and chef of the Fourth Street Grill, known for its mesquite-grilled fish.

ELISABETH THORSTENSSON

A native of northern Sweden, Elisabeth Thorstensson grew up in a family of ardent cooks. After she emigrated to the United States, she worked for a Swedish diplomat at the United Nations and later as a private cook for Mary Martin at her Brazilian ranch. Currently, she is the chef for the executive dining room at a major corporation in New York City.

LINDA JOHNSON

As a practicing nutritionist, Linda Johnson teaches overweight people new eating habits. She is founder and director of *Mind over Matter*, a nutrition and weight management program in the San Francisco Bay area, and is an active member of the American Heart Association. She has also been a contributing nutrition editor for *Women's Sports* and *Glamour* magazine. Her husband, Robert Umbdenstock, collaborated with her in planning the menus for this volume.

Fish and Shellfish in Minutes

GREAT MEALS FOR FOUR, IN AN HOUR OR LESS

As the nineteenth-century French gastronome Brillat-Savarin wrote in *The Physiology of Taste*, "...fish in the hands of a skilled cook can become an inexhaustable source of gustatory pleasures..." The same can be said of shellfish. Whether boiled, broiled, fried, baked, poached, served hot or cold, fish and shellfish are indispensable to creative cooks, especially to those in a hurry. Unlike beef or pork, fish never requires long, slow cooking. Almost all fish and shellfish are naturally tender; overcooking dries them out.

Fish and shellfish are two very different forms of aquatic life. A fish is a vertebrate, an animal with a backbone that propels itself by means of fins and breathes with gills. The term *shellfish* applies to certain edible mollusks and crustaceans. All shellfish are invertebrates, animals that lack a backbone and most often have some kind of shell. Crustaceans, which have jointed feet and a hard external skeleton, include lobsters, shrimps, prawns, crabs, and crayfishes. Mollusks that are enclosed in a hard shell include clams, mussels, oysters, and scallops. Mollusks that have an internal shell or no shell at all, include octopuses, squids, and cuttlefishes.

Scientists estimate that fish and shellfish evolved about 450 million years ago. Seafood was probably humanity's first game food; fish are relatively easy to capture by hand, to stun with a club, or to spear. Gathering shellfish is easier still, as enormous ancient mounds of discarded shells indicate. Scattered along coastal regions throughout the world, these piles show that people quickly discovered the diversity of shellfish—from mussels and clams to oysters, snails, and abalone. With more sophisticated equipment—hooks and lines, nets, traps, and scooping devices—primitive peoples ventured out on boats from coastal areas and river banks to explore the abundant marine life in deeper waters.

Traditionally, Americans have been meat eaters, yet regional cooks have created their own seafood specialties: New England clam chowder, San Francisco *cioppino*, Maryland crab cakes, and New Orleans shrimp Creole, to name a few. And many social occasions focus on fish:

A basket of unopened mussels and hard-shell clams await the cookpot; a platter of clams on the half shell are ready for serving. Arrayed on a bed of crushed ice, with whole lemons and parsley sprigs, are several varieties of fish and shellfish (clockwise, from top left): sea scallops, red snapper, brook trout, raw oysters on the half shell, cooked lobster, salmon steaks, fresh squid, and shrimp.

clambakes, oyster roasts, fish fries, clamming parties, and nighttime grunion runs.

Because of its nutritional value, seafood is increasingly popular. Low-calorie fish protein contains a well-balanced mixture of essential amino acids. In general, most fish and shellfish are low in fat and low in sodium (even though ocean fish live in a salty environment), and contain magnesium, phosphorus, potassium, iron, and certain trace minerals. Saltwater fish also contain relatively large amounts of iodine, another dietary essential. Thus, fish is an ideal food for the health-conscious cook as well as the busy one.

On the following pages, nine of America's most talented cooks present 27 complete menus featuring fish and shellfish. Every menu can be made in an hour or less, and the cooks focus on a new kind of American cuisine that borrows ideas and techniques from around the world but also values our native traditions. They use fresh produce, with no powdered sauces or other dubious shortcuts. The other ingredients (vinegars, spices, herbs, and so on) are all high quality yet available for the most part in supermarkets or, occasionally, in a specialty shop. Each of the menus serves four people and includes other dishes that work well with fish or shellfish.

The photographs accompanying each meal show exactly how the dishes will look when you bring them to the table. The cooks and the test kitchen have planned the meals for appearance as well as taste: The vegetables are brilliant and fresh, the visual combinations appetizing. The table settings feature bright colors, simple flower arrangements, and attractive, but not necessarily expensive, serving pieces. You can readily adapt your own tableware to these menus in convenient ways that will please you and your guests.

For each menu, the Editors, with advice from the cooks, suggest wines and other beverages. And there are suggestions for the best uses of leftovers and for appropriate desserts. On each menu page, too, you will find a range of other tips, from the best way to seed and chop a hot pepper to tricks for selecting the freshest produce. All the recipes have been tested meticulously to make sure that even a relatively inexperienced cook can complete them within the time limit.

BEFORE YOU START

Great Meals in Minutes is designed for efficiency and ease. The books will work best for you when you follow these suggestions:

SAFETY NOTES

Cooking at high temperatures can be dangerous, but not if you follow a few simple steps:

▶ Water added to hot fat will always cause spattering. If possible, pat foods dry with a cloth or paper towel before you add them to the hot oil in a skillet, Dutch oven, or wok.

▶ Lay the food in the pan gently, or the fat will certainly spatter.

▶ Be aware of your cooking environment. If you are boiling or steaming some foods while sautéing others, place the pots far enough apart so the water is unlikely to splash into the oil.

▶ Turn pot handles inward, toward the middle of the stove, so that you do not accidentally knock something over.

▶ Remember that alcohol—wine, brandy, or spirits—may occasionally catch fire when you add it to a very hot pan. If this happens, stand back for your own protection, and then quickly cover the pan with a lid. The fire will instantly subside, and the food will be just as good as ever.

▶ Keep pot holders and mitts close enough to be handy, but never hang them above the burners and do not lay them on the stove top.

1. Read the guidelines (pages 8–9) for selecting fish and shellfish.

2. Refresh your memory on the few simple cooking techniques on the following pages. They will quickly become second nature and will help you produce professional meals in minutes.

3. Read the menus *before* you shop. Each one opens with a list of all the required ingredients, listed in the order you would expect to shop for them in the average supermarket. Check for those few you need to buy; many items will already be on your pantry shelf.

4. Check the equipment list on page 15. A good, sharp knife or knives and pots and pans of the right shape and material are essential for making great meals in minutes. This may be the time to look critically at what you own and to plan to buy a few things. The right equipment can turn cooking from a necessity into a creative experience.

5. Get out everything you need before you start to cook: The lists at the beginning of each menu tell just what is required. To save effort, keep your ingredients close at hand and always put them in the same place so you can reach for them instinctively.

6. Take your meat, fish, and dairy products from the refrigerator early enough for them to come to room temperature and thereby cut cooking time.

7. Follow the step-by-step game plan with each menu. That way, you can be sure of having the entire meal ready to serve at the right moment.

SELECTING SEAFOOD

Twentieth-century technology—refrigeration, freezing, and canning—permits mass marketing of seafood. Approximately 250 varieties of fishes and shellfishes are now sold commercially in the United States. Many of these, particularly freshwater fishes, are familiar only to consumers in the regions where they are caught.

All seafood is highly perishable, so freshness is paramount. But, unlike meat and poultry, fish and shellfish is not subject to mandatory federal or state inspection. A very limited amount of fresh fish and shellfish is inspected by the U.S. Department of Commerce inspectors. Therefore, all consumers should learn to recognize and select fresh seafood. Read the guidelines on the following pages and, if the specified seafood is unavailable or not of satisfactory quality, use the seafood listing to substitute the best alternative.

In addition to checking for freshness, the consumer should remember that, in some states, contaminated freshwater fish may be unsafe for consumption by children, pregnant women, and women of child-bearing age. For information on local guidelines, consult your state authorities. Consumers who collect their own shellfish should also bear in mind that they can be taken only from clean water, or they may contain potentially dangerous bacteria or viruses.

JUDGING FRESHNESS

To choose prime fish, use these tips. The eyes will be shiny and bulging; the gills will be bright red, not brown or rust-colored; and the skin moist and shiny. Fresh fish will feel firm and elastic to the touch, not flabby or soft. Cut up or filleted, fish should look moist; avoid dried-out or discolored pieces. Fresh fish has a mild, sweetish, clean aroma and never smells "fishy," sour, or of ammonia. However, sharks, rays, and skates smell of ammonia for two days after being caught, and then the smell disappears.

Select your fish dealer carefully. Not every retail store sells reliably fresh seafood. A good store will be odor-free and display all its fresh fish on beds of crushed ice. Many supermarkets sell fresh fish already packaged, and some date the package. After buying the fish, check the freshness of your purchase by opening the package before you leave the market. If the fish smells tainted, ask for a refund or an exchange.

Freshness is just as critical for shellfish. All species spoil quickly out of the water. Many shellfish are kept alive until you are ready to cook or eat them. For example, live lobsters, kept in tanks of sea water, should be energetic and curl their tails when lifted. Crabs should move in a lively way. Fresh raw shrimps will vary in color according to their origin but will be greenish-grey or pinkish. The flesh will feel firm and slippery. Cooked shrimps are pinkish-white.

Some shellfish, such as live oysters, mussels, and hard-shell clams, are displayed on beds of crushed ice and keep their shells tightly closed when out of the water. Any with even slightly open shells may be old or dead and must be discarded. In addition, discard any that feel unusually light or heavy in the shell. Shucked bivalves should look plump and uniform in color. Soft-shell (steamer) clams are sold live and retract their siphon when touched. Squid and octopus are never sold live but, like all fresh shellfish, should have fresh-looking, moist flesh and no disagreeable sour fish odor. Squid should have creamy-white flesh, partially covered with the patchy mauve skin.

WHAT TO LOOK FOR IN THE MARKET

A fish dealer cuts a fish according to its size, shape, and intended use. Flat fish, such as flounder, are usually sold whole, pan dressed (without head or tail), or as fillets, although large flat fish, like halibut, may be cut into steaks. Round fish, such as trout, are sold whole, pan dressed, in steaks and fillets.

Fish

Fresh fish is marketed in these easy-to-identify forms:

Whole: The fish is whole, as it comes from the water. It may have been scaled but will need to be gutted.

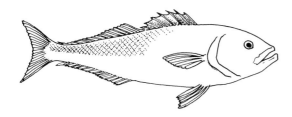

Drawn: The fish is whole and has been gutted and scaled. Whole fish may be baked, grilled, steamed, poached, or fried.

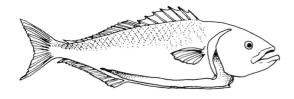

Dressed or pan-dressed: The fish is whole but its head, tail, fins, scales, and viscera have been removed. Small pan-dressed fish are usually sautéed or deep fried.

Butterfly fillets: The fish, round or flat, has been cut into boneless twin fillets that are attached to each other by a strip of uncut skin along the back of the fish. The fillets are opened out and cooked as for ordinary fillets.

Fillets: The fish has been cut lengthwise, along the backbone, into boneless, skinless pieces. These delicate cuts can be cooked by any method but usually need moist heat because they tend to dry out quickly.

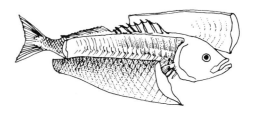

Steaks: The fish, a large dressed round fish has been cut into crosswise sections about 1 to 1½ inches thick. The backbone and skin have not been removed. Steaks can be cooked by any method but need added moisture if prepared by dry-heat cooking.

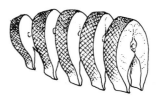

Sticks and portions: The fish has been cut into steaks or fillets, which are then frozen and cut into uniform pieces. They are usually breaded and fried.

Shellfish

Fresh shellfish is usually sold in its natural form. Clams and oysters are obtainable either in the shell or shucked. Mussels are sold in the shell, but scallops are almost always sold shucked. Depending on their size, squid may be sold whole or may have been cut into convenient serving portions. Shrimps and prawns are sold both raw and cooked, shelled and unshelled, and frequently the head has been removed.

CLEANING AND DRESSING FISH

Although most supermarkets and retail fish stores sell fresh fish already drawn or dressed, good cooks should know how to prepare their own fresh fish.

With a few exceptions, such as eel and trout, fish require scaling, which is done with a knife or special implement. First, rinse the fish in cold water, then lay the wet fish on a flat surface. Grasp the tail with one hand and hold a sharp knife vertically (perpendicular to the fish) in the other. Scrape off the scales with the blunt side of the blade from tail end forward, in short, firm strokes.

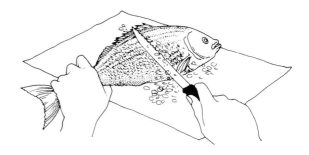

Round fish

To gut a round fish, use a sharp knife to slit open the stomach from the head to the vent (located about one-third the length of the fish anterior to the tail), then pull out the viscera (see illustration below). Remove the blood line, at the base of the backbone, and clean the cavity to remove the membrane by rubbing with a little coarse salt. For a flat fish, make a small cut in the belly behind the gills and pull out the viscera.

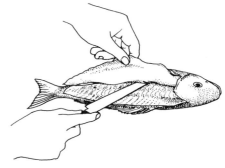

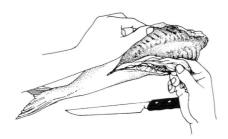

If you plan to cook any fish whole, you must remove the tough, bitter gills: Reach through the gill opening and pull out the gills. If you wish to remove the head, cut straight down behind the gills. Cut away the fins for easier cooking and eating and for a more attractive presentation. However, if poaching, leave the top and bottom fins, as they help to hold the fish together. Rinse the cleaned fish well inside and out, under cold running water, carefully removing any remaining scales. Pat it dry with paper towels.

Whole fish and steaks are almost always cooked with their skin intact, but for fillets, you will usually remove both skin and bones. To fillet a round fish, place the cleaned fish, with or without the head, on a flat surface, with the head pointing away from you. With a long sharp flexible-blade knife, slice through the flesh from just behind the head to the tail to expose the backbone. Next, just behind the gill, slice straight down to the backbone. Grasping the head with one hand and holding the knife horizontally, insert the knife at the head and slice the flesh away from the backbone in short strokes. Then, lift off the whole side of the fish in one piece (see illustration below). Turn the fish over and repeat this process on the other side. Run your fingertips along the inside of the fillet to check for any remaining bones: Remove the larger ones with your fingers, the smaller ones with tweezers. To skin the fillets, lay the fillet, skin side down, on a flat surface. Insert the knife blade between the skin and the flesh at the tail end, and carefully slice the skin off of the flesh. Repeat the process with the other fillet.

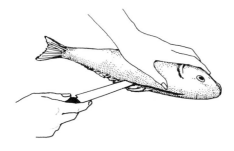

Flat fish

Flat fish are usually skinned before being filleted. To skin, make a shallow cut in the skin at the tail. Then, hold the tail firmly in one hand and, grasping the skin tightly with the other, peel it off of the fish. Repeat the process on the other side. To fillet a flat fish, with or without the head, lay the fish on a flat surface. Insert the knife tip at the head end and cut along the backbone to the tail. Slip the blade under the flesh, and gently cut the flesh away from the bones, working from head to tail, to remove the fillet in one piece. Cut away the second fillet in the same way, and then turn the fish over and repeat the process on the other side (see illustration below). You will have four fillets.

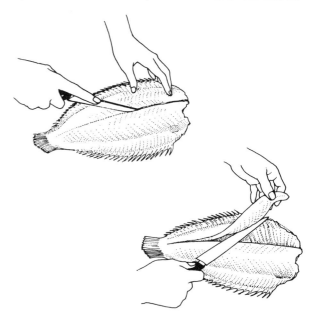

HANDLING SHELLFISH

You may wish to purge bivalves (clams, mussels, and oysters). To do this, place the live bivalves, in their shells, in a gallon of cold water with one teaspoon of sea salt and one cup of cornmeal, and let sit for at least 3 hours.

Clams: With a stiff brush, scrub the clams under cold running water to remove any surface mud. To shuck, hold the clam over a bowl to catch the liquor and insert the blade of a clam knife or a wide, rounded-end blade between the shells opposite the hinge. Twist the blade to force the shell halves apart, then slide the cutting edge of the blade along the inside to cut apart the muscles holding the shells together.

Mussels: With a stiff brush, scrub the mussels under cold running water to remove any surface mud. Remove

Seafood for This Volume

The fish and shellfish listed below are called for in this volume; however, many of the cooks specify substitutions. If even the specified substitute is unavailable, you can usually substitute another fish and still get good results, whether it is a fresh or salt water fish.

For some shellfish recipes, you can substitute within the same zoological family. For example, blue crab is not exactly like a Dungeness crab in size, color, or flavor but will be similar enough.

FISH

Cod: Atlantic cod and Pacific cod have lean, firm white flesh. Cod may be called scrod when weighing less than two and a half pounds. Related fish may be substituted: haddock, whiting (silver hake), and pollock. Available fresh or frozen, whole, in steaks, and in fillets.

Flatfish: Flounders and halibuts. Some flatfish are called sole. Flatfish have lean, delicately flavored white flesh; some species are firmer-fleshed than others. Related fish may be substituted: summer flounder (fluke); yellowtail flounder; petrale, lemon, gray, and rex soles; halibut; and turbot. Available fresh or frozen, whole, in steaks, and in fillets.

Haddock: See cod. Lean, delicately flavored white flesh.

Halibut: See flatfishes. Fine texture and flavor.

Mackerel: Mackerel, bonito, wahoo. Mackerel has both dark and light fatty flesh. King mackerel is stronger flavored and fattier than Spanish mackerel. Related fish may be substituted: wahoo; bullet, chub, king, Spanish mackerels; and tunas. Another substitute is mullet, a good food fish, found in fresh and salt water. Mackerel is available fresh or frozen, whole, in steaks and in fillets.

Goosefish: Also known as monkfish or angler fish, it has firm, white flesh that tastes like lobster. The only good substitute is the more delicate cusk, related to cod, but both fish are restricted to the Atlantic coast. Only the tail section of goosefish is edible; it is usually marketed without the head.

Red snapper: Flavorful, lean, juicy white flesh. Substitutes are other varieties of snapper on the Pacific coast, or rockfishes. Red snapper is available fresh or frozen, whole and in fillets.

Salmon: Pink, chum, sockeye, and Atlantic salmons have fatty, distinctively-flavored firm flesh that ranges in color from white to deep coral. There is no substitute for salmon. It is available fresh or frozen, whole, in fillets, and in steaks.

Sea bass: Lean, firm, white flesh. Related fish may be substituted: black sea bass, sand perch, groupers, scamp, sand bass, and striped bass. Sea bass is available fresh, whole and in fillets.

Shark: Mako. It has texture, color, and taste similar to those of swordfish. Related fish may be substituted: porbeagle and blue sharks. Available fresh in steaks, and in fillets.

Sole: See flatfish. All true sole (Dover sole) marketed in the United States is imported from Europe.

Swordfish: Coarse-textured, rich, delicately flavored. Mako shark may be substituted. Available fresh or frozen, in steaks.

Trout: Brook and rainbow; hatchery-bred most commonly available. Light meat, firm flesh, moderately fatty. They can be used interchangeably. Available fresh or frozen, whole, dressed, boned (with backbone and ribs removed).

Tuna: Several varieties, all have fatty, full-flavored, light or dark flesh. Related fish may be substituted: bonito and mackerels. Available fresh or frozen, in steaks.

Whiting (silver hake): See cod. Tender, lean, flaky flesh. Sold fresh or frozen, whole, dressed, or filleted.

SHELLFISH

Crab: Hard-shell crabs: blue, rock, Dungeness. Varieties differ from coast to coast, but the meat is delicate and moderately sweet. Available live, fresh, frozen, or cooked.

Lobster: Firm, rich-tasting, non-fatty succulent flesh. Available whole, live, cooked or frozen.

Shrimp and prawns (jumbo shrimp): Delicate, firm flesh. Available fresh, cooked, or frozen, whole, in shell, or shelled.

Clams: Hardshell: littleneck, cherrystone, and chowder clams; softshell. Tender, sweet flesh. Available whole or shucked, fresh or frozen.

Mussels: Mollusks. Tender, sweet flesh. Low fat, high protein. Available live.

Oysters: Tender flesh, with delicate flavor. Low fat, high protein. Available year-round, whole or shucked, fresh and frozen.

Scallops: Bay and sea. Both are tender, with delicately flavored ivory flesh. Available shucked, rarely whole, fresh or frozen.

Squid: Delicately flavored, firm (almost chewy) white flesh. Available whole or cut into pieces, fresh or frozen.

---

the beard and pull off any strands that stick out of the shell. Using a scrubbing brush or knife, scrape off any surface encrustations.

Oysters: With a stiff brush, scrub the oysters under cold running water. To shuck, hold the oyster, with the flatter shell upmost, over a bowl to catch the liquor and insert the tip of an oyster knife into the hinge. Twist the knife to open the shells, then slide the knife along the inside of the upper shell to cut the muscle. Discard the upper shell. To cut the oyster loose from the bottom shell, slice the knife blade under the oyster.

Shrimps and prawns: These are usually sold without the head, but if they are whole, twist off the head. To peel and devein, starting at the head end, slip your thumb under the shell between the feelers. Lift off two or three shell segments at once and, holding the tail, pull the shrimp out of the shell. If desired, pull off the tail shell, or leave it on for a decorative appearance. With a sharp paring knife, slit down the back, and lift out the black vein.

Lobsters: For fresh lobsters, rinse briefly under cold running water prior to cooking.

Squid: Hold the head with one hand, the body with the

other, and firmly pull the head away from the body. Cut off the tentacles and discard the remainder of the head. Pull the transparent quill-like piece out of the body sac and discard it. Wash the squid thoroughly inside and out, and peel the skin away from the body and fins. Slice the body into rings, if desired.

STORING FRESH SEAFOOD

Fresh seafood should always be a last-minute purchase. Fresh fish should be drawn (cleaned) before being stored. Remove all blood, rinse the fish under cold water, and pat it dry with paper towels. Fish will keep best whole. Cover the fish loosely with plastic wrap. If you can provide drainage, store the fish in the refrigerator on ice. Otherwise, store the fish, preferably on an aluminum tray or a plate to maintain an even cold temperature, in the coldest part of your refrigerator.

Fresh bivalves may be stored shucked or unshucked. If storing them in the shell, keep them dry and do not store them on ice. For shucked, store them in their liquor in a closed container, preferably set on ice. Store all shellfish in the coldest part of your refrigerator.

COOKING FISH

Fat content varies from species to species, even within a species, depending on season and diet. As a general rule of thumb, the broad categories "fat" and "lean" help consumers select the right catch at their fish dealer's. Fatty fish (with a fat content ranging from 5 percent to 25 percent) include tunas, salmons, mackerels, and anchovies. Lean fish (those with less than 5 percent fat) include snappers, soles, flounders, and sea basses as well as lobsters, shrimps, and scallops. Because of the difference in fat content and fish size, all cooking techniques are not suitable for all fishes. To some extent, the amount of fat determines the best cooking method: Fattier fish are less likely to become dry when cooked by direct high heat, as in broiling, grilling, and baking. Follow the simple guidelines below to help you select the right technique.

Poaching and steaming: For firm-fleshed fish, because fatty or soft-fleshed fish tend to fall apart in liquid.

Braising and stewing: For firm-fleshed fish, which will not fall apart. Fish fillets are too delicate, but thick steaks are suitable. Avoid strong-tasting fish that may overpower the other ingredients in a mixed dish.

Baking, broiling, and barbecuing: For fatty fish, which retain the internal moisture necessary for dry-heat cooking. However, any type of fish, properly moistened, can be cooked by these methods.

Deep frying, stir frying, sautéing, pan frying: For lean, firm-fleshed fishes, which will hold together and not become too oily. Oily fish may become too rich when fried.

The Canadian Department of Fisheries has devised a simple, foolproof guide for calculating the cooking time for fish: Measure the fish (whole, fillet, or steak) at its thickest part. For fresh fish, cook it 10 minutes for every inch of thickness; for frozen, 20 minutes. This applies to any cooking technique for fish but not for shellfish. However, check for doneness frequently, particularly when broiling

thin fillets. Insert the tip of a sharp knife into the fish: The fish is just cooked when the flesh barely flakes, is opaque, and does not cling to the bones.

COOKING TECHNIQUES

Sautéing

Sautéing is a form of quick frying with no cover on the pan. In French, *sauter* means "to jump," which is what vegetables or small pieces of food do when you shake the sauté pan. The purpose is to lightly brown the food and seal in the juices, sometimes before further cooking. This technique has three critical elements: the right pan, the proper temperature, and dry food.

The sauté pan: A proper sauté pan is 10 to 12 inches in diameter and has 2- to 3-inch straight sides that allow you to turn food pieces and still keep the fat from spattering. It has a heavy bottom that slides easily over a burner.

The best material (and the most expensive) for a sauté pan is tin-lined copper because it is a superior heat conductor. Heavy-gauge aluminum works well but will discolor acidic food like tomatoes. Therefore, you should not use aluminum if the food is to be cooked for more than 20 minutes after the initial browning. Another option is to select a heavy-duty sauté pan made of strong, heat-conductive aluminum alloys. This type of professional cookware is smooth and stick-resistant.

Select a sauté pan large enough to hold the pieces of food without crowding. The heat of the fat and the air spaces around and between the pieces facilitate browning. Crowding results in steaming—a technique that lets the juices out rather than sealing them in. If your sauté pan is not large enough to prevent crowding, separate the food into two batches, or use two pans at once.

Be sure you buy a sauté pan with a tight-fitting cover. Many recipes call for sautéing first, then lowering the heat and cooking the food, covered, for an additional 10 to 20 minutes. Make certain the handle is long and is comfortable to hold.

Never immerse the hot pan in cold water because this will warp the metal. Allow the pan to cool slightly, then add water and let it sit until you are ready to wash it. Use a wooden spatula or tongs to keep food pieces moving in the pan as you shake it over the burner. If the food sticks, as it occasionally will, a metal spatula will loosen it best. Turn the pieces so that all surfaces come into contact with the hot fat and none of them sticks. Do not use a fork when sautéing meat; piercing the meat will toughen it.

The fat: A combination of half butter and half vegetable oil or peanut oil is perfect for most sautéing: it heats to high temperatures without burning and allows you to have a rich butter flavor at the same time. Always use unsalted butter for cooking, since it tastes better and does not add unwanted salt to your recipe.

Butter alone makes a wonderful-tasting sauté, but butter, whether salted or unsalted, burns at a high temperature. If you prefer an all-butter flavor, clarify the butter before you begin. This means removing the milky residue, which is the part that scorches. To clarify butter,

Making Stocks

Although canned chicken broth or stock is all right for emergencies, homemade chicken stock has a rich flavor that is hard to match. Moreover, the commercial broths—particularly the canned ones—are likely to be oversalted.

To make your own stock, save chicken parts as they accumulate and put them in a bag in the freezer; then have a rainy-day stock-making session, using the recipe below. The skin from a yellow onion will add color; the optional veal bone will add extra flavor and richness to the stock.

Basic Chicken Stock

3 pounds bony chicken parts, such as wings, back, and neck
1 veal knuckle (optional)
3 quarts cold water
1 yellow unpeeled onion, stuck with 2 cloves
2 stalks celery with leaves, cut in two
12 crushed peppercorns
2 carrots, scraped and cut into 2-inch lengths
4 sprigs parsley
1 bay leaf
1 tablespoon fresh thyme, or 1 teaspoon dried
Salt (optional)

1. Wash chicken parts and veal knuckle (if you are using it) and drain. Place in large soup kettle or stockpot (any big pot) with the remaining ingredients—except salt. Cover pot and bring to a boil over medium heat.

2. Lower heat and simmer stock, partly covered, 2 to 3 hours. Skim foam and scum from top of stock several times. Add salt to taste after stock has cooked 1 hour.

3. Strain stock through fine sieve placed over large bowl. Discard chicken pieces, vegetables, and seasonings. Let stock cool uncovered (this will speed cooling process). When completely cool, refrigerate. Fat will rise and congeal conveniently at top. You may skim it off and discard it or leave it as protective covering for stock.

Yield: About 10 cups.

Fish stock, also known as fish fumet, is a delicate aromatic broth used as a poaching or braising liquid for fish or as the base of a sauce to be served with fish. Ask your fish dealer to provide you with the day's trimmings, which you may want to request a day in advance. Any unused trimmings may be frozen and used another time. Or, double the stock recipe and refrigerate or freeze the leftover stock in small containers. It will keep up to three days in the refrigerator or up to six months in the freezer.

When making fish stock, be sure to add the salt only after the cooking is finished. The stock is concentrated through reduction and what tastes just right at the beginning of the cooking process may be oversalty by the time the stock is done.

Fish stock should not be cooked for more than 30 minutes or it may acquire an unpleasant taste.

Although fish stock is both easy and quick to make, you may occasionally need to take a shortcut. Bottled clam juice, diluted with water, is an acceptable substitute. Use one part clam juice to one part water and proceed with the recipe as though using fish stock.

Fish Stock

2 pounds fish bones, heads, or tails
½ cup sliced carrots
½ cup sliced onions or shallots
½ cup sliced celery
1 bay leaf
5 to 6 parsley sprigs
7 to 8 peppercorns
2 cups white wine (optional)
Salt

1. Remove the gills and any innards. Cut or break the fish into chunks.
2. In large saucepan, combine fish pieces with carrots, onions, celery, bay leaf, parsley, peppercorns, wine, if using, and 6 cups cold water if using wine, 8 cups if not.
3. Bring mixture to a boil over high heat, reduce to a simmer, and cook, uncovered, about 30 minutes, skimming as necessary. Stock should reduce by about half.
4. Strain stock through fine sieve set over large bowl. If stock has not reduced by half, return it to saucepan and bring to a boil over high heat. Reduce to a simmer and cook, uncovered, until reduction is completed. Add salt to taste.
5. Leave stock to cool, uncovered, and then pour into containers and store.

heat it in a small saucepan over medium heat and, using a cooking spoon, skim off the foam as it rises to the top and discard it. Keep skimming until no more foam appears. Pour off the remaining oil, making sure to leave the milky residue at the bottom of the pan. The oil is clarified butter; use this for sautés. It is a simple matter to make a large quantity of it and store it in your refrigerator; it will keep for two to three weeks. Some sautéing recipes in this book call for olive oil, which imparts a delicious and distinctive flavor and is less sensitive than butter to high heat. Nevertheless, even the finest olive oil has some residue of fruit pulp, which will scorch over high heat. Discard any scorched oil and start with fresh if necessary.

To sauté properly, heat the sauté fat until it is hot but not smoking. When you see small bubbles on top of the fat, it is almost hot enough to smoke. In that case, lower the heat. When using butter and oil together, add the butter to the hot oil. After the foam from the melting butter subsides, you are ready to sauté. If the temperature is just right, the food will sizzle when you put it in.

Steaming

A fast and nutritious way to cook vegetables, steaming is also an excellent method for cooking meat or fish. Bring water, or a combination of stock and wine, to a boil in a steamer. Place the food in the steaming-basket or rack over the liquid, and cover the pan—periodically checking the water level. Keeping the food above the liquid preserves vitamins and minerals. Kathleen Sanderson (pages 76–77) steams potatoes for her potato salad.

Frozen Fish

Even for those who live near lakes and oceans, frozen fish and shellfish are sometimes the only option. Because commercial freezing methods have improved in recent years, frozen fish can be perfectly palatable, and many varieties are available.

When buying frozen fish in a package, check that the package is airtight and frozen solid. Stored at 0 degrees Fahrenheit, fatty fish last for up to 3 months; lean fish, up to 6 months. Keep the frozen seafood in its original wrapping until you are ready to cook it. When you open the package, check to see that there are no ice crystals. The seafood should look firm, with no signs of freezer burn (white patches or discolorations), and should not have a rancid, fishy smell. To avoid any problems, do not buy any packages that are misshapen, have torn wrappings, or show traces of blood.

Commercially frozen fish and shellfish are processed immediately after they have been caught and are at their peak of freshness and quality. However, freezing seafood at home is not recommended, as home freezers do not freeze seafood fast enough to maintain freshness. If you wish to freeze fresh fish at home, do not use store-bought fish unless you know that it is freshly caught. Freeze only drawn (cleaned) fish, remove all blood, and wrap it airtight to preserve moisture and freshness. Use plastic wrap or plastic bags rather than foil for packaging, because plastic fits and seals more tightly and thus prevents freezer burn. Seal and date each package. To freeze mollusks, shuck them and store them in their liquor in a freezer container. Scallops toughen when frozen. If freezing at home, lobster, crab, and shrimp should be cooked first. Squid and octopus should be cleaned and then frozen whole or cut up.

Thawing fish: Fillets, steaks, and dressed fish can be cooked frozen, as long as you allow a few extra minutes of cooking time. Whole fish needs thawing: If you are in a hurry, you can thaw it, wrapped in the original package, under cold water. Otherwise, thaw it in the refrigerator for 24 hours. Never thaw fish at room temperature; it will become soggy. Never refreeze thawed fish.

The following recipes in this volume have been tested using a frozen fish substitute: frozen halibut for the fresh shark in Leslie Land's Menu 2 (see pages 23–24); frozen perch for the fresh trout in Kathleen Sanderson's Menu 2 (page 73); frozen cod for the sole in Josephine Araldo's Menu 2 (page 53); frozen shrimp for fresh shrimp (prawns) in Linda Johnson's Menu 1 (pages 96–97); frozen sole for fresh sole in Elisabeth Thorstensson's Menu 1 (page 89).

Stir Frying

This basic cooking method for Chinese cuisine requires very little oil, and the foods—which you stir continuously—fry quickly over very high heat. It is ideal for cooking bite-size, shredded, or thinly sliced portions of vegetables, fish, meat, or poultry. Bruce Cliborne (page 67) uses this cooking method for his Clams in Sesame-Ginger Sauce.

Braising

This method cooks food by moist heat, but you generally brown the food well before combining it with the cooking liquid. Then you simmer the food and the liquid slowly over low heat. Braising produces delicious vegetable dishes. See Leslie Land's Lemon-Braised Celery, Endive, and Watercress (pages 26–27).

Flambéing

Flambéing requires igniting an already-warm, but not close to boiling, liqueur in the pan with already-cooked hot food. Be sure to remove the pan from the heat first; then avert your face and ignite the liqueur with a lighted match. A quiet flame will burn for a few seconds. Linda Johnson uses this method for her Prawns with Green Peppercorns (pages 96–97). Allow about an ounce of liqueur per person. The taste remains, but the alcohol burns off.

Poaching

You poach meat, fish, or chicken, even fruit, exactly as you would an egg, in very hot liquid in a shallow pan on top of the stove. You can use water, or better still, beef, chicken, or fish stock, or a combination of stock and white wine, or even cream. Bring the liquid to the simmering point and add the food. Be prepared to lower the heat if the liquid begins to boil. See Mark Miller's Poached Oysters with Saffron Cream Sauce (page 85).

Blanching

Blanching, also called parboiling, is an invaluable technique. Immerse whole or cut vegetables for a few moments in boiling water, then "refresh" them—that is, plunge them in cold water to stop their cooking and set their colors. Blanching softens or tenderizes dense or crisp vegetables, often as a preliminary to further cooking by another method, such as stir frying.

Broiling and Grilling

These are two relatively fast ways to cook meat, poultry and fish, giving the food a crisp exterior while leaving the inside juicy. For uniform cooking, flatten the pieces of food to an even thickness. Whether broiling or grilling, brush fish with melted fat, a sauce, or marinade before you cook. This adds flavor and keeps the food moist.

In broiling, the meat cooks directly under the heat source. To ensure proper cooking, move the broiling rack five or six inches from the heat source.

Roasting and Baking

Originally, *roasting* was the term for cooking meat on a revolving spit over an open fire, but now it means cooking meat or poultry in an oven by a dry-heat process. Roasting is especially suitable for thick cuts of meat and whole poultry. You should baste food several times with dripping or a flavorful basting sauce.

Baking also means cooking food in the oven, but it is a much more versatile technique. You use it for preparing breads and raw vegetables or for cooking a combination of foods. Also, you use this technique for salt baking, that is, burying fish, meat, or poultry in coarse salt as with Patricia Unterman's Trout Baked in Coarse Salt (page 47); and for parchment baking, that is, wrapping food in kitchen parchment. See Patricia Unterman's Fish Baked in Parchment with Red Peppers (pages 43–44).

Equipment

Proper cooking equipment makes the work light and is a good cook's most prized possession. You can cook expertly without a store-bought steamer or even a food processor, but basic pans, knives, and a few other items are indispensable. Below are the things you need—and some attractive options—for preparing the menus in this volume.

Pots and pans
Large kettle or stockpot
3 skillets (large, medium, small), with covers
2 sauté pans, 10 to 12 inches in diameter, with covers and oven-proof handles
3 saucepans with covers (1-, 2-, and 4-quart capacities)
  Choose enameled cast-iron, plain cast-iron, aluminum-clad stainless steel, and heavy aluminum (but you need at least one saucepan that is not aluminum). Best—but very expensive—is tin-lined copper.
Roasting pan
Broiler pan
3 shallow baking pans (8 x 8 x 2-inch, 13 x 9 x 2-inch, and 15 x 17 x 2-inch)
2 cookie sheets (11 x 17-inch and 15½ x 12-inch)
18-inch jelly-roll pan
2-quart soufflé dish
2- or 3-quart casserole with cover
7 x 12-inch flameproof baking dish
Set of heatproof baking dishes
Four ½-cup ramekins
9-inch or 10-inch pie plate
2 cake pans (9-inch diameter)
Platter

Knives
  A carbon-steel knife takes a sharp edge but tends to rust. You must wash and dry it after each use; otherwise it can blacken foods and counter tops. Good-quality stainless steel knives, frequently honed, are less trouble and will serve just as well in the home kitchen. Never put a fine knife in the dishwasher. Rinse it, dry it, and put it away—but not loose in a drawer. Knives will stay sharp and last a long time if they have their own storage rack.
Small paring knife (sharp-pointed end)
10-inch chef's knife
Sharpening steel

Other cooking tools
2 sets of mixing bowls in graduated sizes

Flour sifter
Colander, with a round base (stainless steel, aluminum, or enamel)
Strainers (preferably 2, in fine and coarse mesh)
Sieve, coarse and fine mesh
2 sets of measuring cups and spoons in graduated sizes
  One for dry ingredients, another for shortenings and liquids.
Long-handled cooking spoon
Long-handled slotted spoon
3 long-handled wooden spoons
Long-handled, 2-pronged fork
Wooden spatula (for stirring hot ingredients)
Metal spatula, or turner (for lifting hot foods from pans)
Slotted spatula
Rubber or vinyl spatula (for folding in ingredients)
Grater (metal, with several sizes of holes)
  A rotary grater is handy for hard cheese.
2 wire whisks
Pair of metal tongs
Wooden chopping board
Food mill, ricer, or potato masher
Vegetable steamer
Vegetable peeler
Mortar and pestle
Soup ladle
Four 8- to 10-inch metal or bamboo skewers
Nutcracker
Kitchen scissors
Kitchen timer
Stiff scrubbing brush
Kitchen string
Toothpicks
Aluminum foil
Cheesecloth
Paper towels
Plastic wrap
Wax paper
Thin rubber gloves

Electric appliances
Food processor or blender

A blender will do most of the work required in this volume, but a food processor will do it more quickly and in larger volume. A food processor should be considered a necessity, not a luxury, for anyone who enjoys cooking.
Electric mixer

Optional
Wok
Double boiler
Steamer unit
Gratin dish
Copper bowl
Salad spinner
Bread knife (serrated edge)
Fish scaling knife or implement
Fish filleting knife
Clam or oyster knife
Chinese wok spatulas
Citrus juicer
  Inexpensive glass kind from the dime store will do.
Melon baller
Pastry brush for basting
  A small, new paintbrush that is not nylon serves well.
Rolling pin
Flametamer or asbestos mat
Garlic press
Zester
Baking parchment
Roll of masking tape or white paper tape for labeling and dating

Pantry (for this volume)

A well-stocked, properly organized pantry is essential for preparing great meals in the shortest time possible. Whether your pantry consists of a small refrigerator and two or three shelves over the sink, or a large freezer, refrigerator, and entire room just off the kitchen, you must protect staples from heat and light.

In maintaining your pantry, follow these rules:

1. Store staples by kind and date. Canned goods, canisters, and spices need a separate shelf, or a separate spot on a shelf. Date all staples—shelved, refrigerated, or frozen—by writing the date directly on the package or on a bit of masking tape. Then put the oldest ones in front to be sure you use them first.

2. Store flour, sugar, and other dry ingredients in canisters or jars with tight lids. Glass and clear plastic allow you to see at a glance how much remains.

3. Keep a running grocery list so that you can note when a staple is half gone, and be sure to stock up.

ON THE SHELF:

Baking powder

Baking soda

Capers

Capers are usually packed in vinegar and less frequently in salt. If you use the latter, you should rinse them under cold water before using them.

Clam juice, bottled

May be substituted for fish stock. Be careful to add it gradually; it is very salty and may need to be diluted.

Cornstarch

Less likely to lump than flour, cornstarch is an excellent thickener for sauces. Substitute in the following proportions: 1 tablespoon cornstarch to 2 of flour.

Crème fraîche, homemade, or commercial.

Dried fruits

currants

raisins, dark and golden

Flour

all-purpose, bleached or unbleached

cornmeal

May be yellow or white and of various degrees of coarseness. The stone-ground variety, milled to retain the germ of the corn, generally has a superior flavor.

Garlic

Store in a cool, dry, well-ventilated place. Garlic powder and garlic salt are not adequate substitutes for fresh garlic.

Herbs and spices

The flavor of fresh herbs is much better than that of dried. Fresh herbs should be refrigerated and used as soon as possible. The following herbs are perfectly acceptable dried, but buy in small amounts, store airtight in dry area away from heat and light, and use as quickly as possible. In measuring herbs, remember that one part dried will equal three parts fresh. *Note:* Dried chives and parsley should not be on your shelf, since they have little or no flavor; frozen chives are acceptable. Buy whole spices rather than ground, as they keep their flavor much longer. Grind spices at home and store as directed for herbs.

anise seeds

basil

bay leaves

Cayenne pepper

celery seeds

chervil

chili peppers, whole and ground

chives

cinnamon, sticks and ground

cloves, whole and ground

coriander

cumin

curry powder, preferably imported

dill

fennel seeds

ginger

juniper berries

marjoram

mint

mustard (powdered)

nutmeg, whole and ground

oregano

paprika

pepper

black peppercorns

These are unripe peppercorns dried in their husks. Grind with a pepper mill for each use.

white peppercorns

These are the same as the black variety, but are picked ripe and husked. Use them in pale sauces when black pepper specks would spoil the appearance.

poppy seeds

red pepper flakes (also called crushed red pepper)

rosemary

saffron

Made from the dried stigmas of a species of crocus, this spice—the most costly of all seasonings—adds both color and flavor.

salt

Use coarse salt—commonly available as Kosher or sea— for its superior flavor, texture, and purity. Kosher salt and sea salt are less salty than table salt. Substitute in the following proportions: three quarters teaspoon table salt equals just under one teaspoon Kosher or sea salt.

sesame seeds

thyme

turmeric

Honey

Jalapeño peppers

Nuts, whole, chopped or slivered

almonds

pecans

pine nuts

walnuts

Oils

corn, safflower, or vegetable

Because these neutral-tasting oils have high smoking points, they are good for high-heat sautéing.

olive oil

Sample French, Greek, Spanish, and Italian oils. Olive oil ranges in color from pale yellow to dark green and in taste from mild and delicate to rich and fruity. Different olive oils can be used for different purposes: for example, lighter ones for cooking, stronger ones for salads. The finest quality olive oil is labeled extra-virgin or virgin.

sesame oil (Chinese and Japanese)

Sold in the Oriental section of most supermarkets, it is almost always used for seasoning. Keeps indefinitely when refrigerated.

walnut oil

Rich and nutty tasting. It turns rancid easily, so keep it tightly closed in the refrigerator.

Onions

Store all dry-skinned onions in a cool, dry, well-ventilated place.

Bermuda onions

Large and mild, with a flattish shape, they are best

baked whole or eaten raw, although they can be used in cooking. They are generally yellow but also may be red or white.

red or Italian onions

Zesty tasting and generally eaten raw. The perfect salad onion.

Spanish onions

Very large with a sweet flavor, they are best for stuffing and baking and are also eaten raw. Perfect for sandwiches.

shallots

The most subtle member of the onion family, the shallot has a delicate garlic flavor.

yellow onions

All-purpose cooking onions, strong in taste.

white onions

Also called boiling onions, these small onions are almost always cooked and served whole.

Pasta and noodles

fettucine, fresh or dried

orzo

Potatoes, boiling and baking

"New" potatoes are not a particular kind of potato, but any potato that has not been stored.

Rice

brown rice

From the same plant as white rice, but the bran, which is not all removed, colors it and gives a subtle, nutlike flavor. Needs longer cooking and more liquid.

long-grain white rice

Slender grains, much longer than they are wide, that become light and fluffy when cooked and are best for general use.

Serrano peppers

Soy sauce

Stock, chicken and fish

For maximum flavor and quality, your own stock is best (see recipes page 13), but canned stock, or broth, is adequate for most recipes and convenient to have on hand.

Sugar

brown sugar

confectioners' sugar

granulated sugar

Tomatoes

Italian plum tomatoes

Canned plum tomatoes (preferably imported) are an acceptable substitute for fresh.

tomato paste

Also for sauces. Spoon single tablespoons of unused canned paste onto wax paper and freeze them. Lift frozen paste off and store in plastic container. Sometimes available in tubes, which can be stored in the refrigerator after a small amount is used.

Vanilla extract

Use pure, not imitation, extract.

Vinegars

apple cider vinegar (also called cider vinegar)

Use for a mild, fruity flavor.

balsamic vinegar

Aged vinegar with a complex sweet and sour taste

red and white wine vinegars

rice vinegar

rice wine vinegar

sherry vinegar

Somewhat less sharp than most wine vinegars, it has a deeper, fuller flavor.

tarragon vinegar

A white wine vinegar flavored with fresh tarragon, it is especially good in salads.

Water chestnuts, canned

Fresh in flavor and crunchy in texture, they are the bulbs of an Asian marsh plant, not chestnuts at all.

Wines and spirits

bourbon

Brandy or Cognac

gin

sherry, sweet and dry

Pernod

vermouth, sweet and dry

white wine, dry

Worcestershire sauce

IN THE REFRIGERATOR:

Bread crumbs

You need never buy bread crumbs. To make fresh crumbs, use fresh or day-old bread and process in food processor or blender. For dried, toast bread 30 minutes in preheated 250-degree oven, turning occasionally to prevent slices from browning. Proceed as for fresh. Store bread crumbs in an airtight container: fresh crumbs in the refrigerator, and dried crumbs in a cool, dry place. Either type may also be frozen for several weeks if tightly wrapped in a plastic bag.

Butter

Many cooks prefer unsalted butter because of its finer flavor and because it does not burn as easily as salted.

Cheese

Parmesan cheese

Avoid the preground packaged variety; it is very expensive and almost flavorless. Buy Parmesan by the quarter- or half-pound wedge and grate as needed: 4 ounces produces about one cup of grated cheese. Romano, far less costly, can be substituted, but its flavor is considerably sharper—or try mixing the two.

Cream

half-and-half

heavy cream

sour cream

Eggs

Will keep 4 to 5 weeks in refrigerator. For best results, bring to room temperature before using.

Ginger, fresh

Found in the produce section. Ginger will stay fresh in the refrigerator for approximately 1 week, wrapped in plastic. To preserve it longer, place the whole ginger root in a small sherry-filled jar; it will last almost indefinitely, although not without changes in the ginger. Or, if you prefer, store it in the freezer, where it will last about 3 months. Newly purchased ginger need not be peeled.

Lemons

In addition to its many uses in cooking, a slice of lemon rubbed over cut apples and pears will keep them from discoloring. Do not substitute bottled juice or lemon extract.

Limes

Mayonnaise

Milk

Mustards

Dry mustard and regular hot dog mustard have their uses and their devotees, but the recipes in this book call for Dijon or coarse-ground mustard.

Parsley

The two most commonly available kinds of parsley are flat-leaved and curly; they can be used interchangeably when necessary. Flat-leaved parsley has a more distinctive flavor and is generally preferred in cooking. Curly parsley wilts less easily and is excellent for garnishing. Store parsley in a glass of water and cover loosely with a plastic bag. It will keep for a week in the refrigerator. Or wash and dry it, and refrigerate in a small plastic bag with a dry paper towel inside to absorb any moisture.

Scallions

Scallions have a mild onion flavor. Store wrapped in plastic.

17

Leslie Land

MENU 1 (Left)
Steamed Lobster with Four Sauces
Sautéed New Cabbage
Oven-Fried Potatoes

MENU 2
Broiled Shark Steaks with Lime-Parsley Sauce
Rice with Walnuts
Broiled Vegetables

MENU 3
Lemon-Braised Celery, Endive, and Watercress
Haddock with Crab Meat and Hazelnut Stuffing

L iving in an isolated coastal area in Maine, Leslie Land does not have the array of ingredients on hand that urban cooks do. But she finds this no hardship. Mail order brings nonperishable goods such as chilies and exotic canned foods, and a fisherman neighbor supplies her with freshly caught seafood. Her two gardens, where she raises four different kinds of strawberries, yield abundant seasonal vegetables, and she gathers her own wild mushrooms.

If seasons and a limited marketplace dictate how and what she cooks, Leslie Land nonetheless enjoys adding the unexpected and unconventional. Menu 1, a summer-fall dinner, features a Maine favorite, steamed lobsters. With them she offers butter sauce, embellished with orange and lemon zests, allspice, and gin. In addition, she offers three other dipping mixtures, not only for the lobsters but also for the fried potatoes and sautéed cabbage. For Menu 3, she stuffs a whole boned and cleaned haddock with ground hazelnuts, crab meat, and currants.

The shark steak entrée of Menu 2 is itself an unusual offering. Shark meat is delicious; steaks from mako sharks, one of the most prevalent varieties sold for food, look and taste like swordfish. Sharks are common in many international dishes: the fish of the British "fish and chips" is often shark. To accompany the shark steaks, Leslie Land serves a nutty brown rice and broiled skewered fresh vegetables.

When you serve this informal company meal, place a boiled lobster and a portion of sautéed cabbage on each guest's plate. Serve the potatoes in a separate container, and set out individual ramekins with the four different dipping sauces within easy reach.

Steamed Lobster with Four Sauces
Sautéed New Cabbage
Oven-Fried Potatoes

Four dipping sauces accompany this meal; they are meant not only for the lobsters but also for the potatoes and cabbage. Two of these sauces are Japanese: one, *tempura*, contains garlic, ginger, and tamari, a rich mellow soy sauce often available in specialty food stores and health food shops. The other, *wasabi* sauce, is made from powdered grated *wasabi*, a strong, nose-tingling green horseradish-like condiment available in Oriental markets and specialty food shops. Regular Western horseradish is not a substitute.

WHAT TO DRINK

Boiled lobster needs a crisp, dry wine; try a California Sauvignon Blanc or Fumé Blanc.

SHOPPING LIST AND STAPLES

4 live "chicken" lobsters (each about 1¼ pounds)
Medium-size head green cabbage (about 1½ pounds)
4 large baking potatoes (about 2½ pounds total weight)
1 bunch fresh dill, or 1 tablespoon dried
Large clove garlic
1-inch piece fresh ginger (about ½ ounce)
Large juice orange
1 lemon
3 to 4 tablespoons milk
1 stick plus 1 tablespoon salted butter
½ pint sour cream
⅓ cup vegetable oil
1 teaspoon cider vinegar or rice vinegar
2 tablespoons tamari or other aged soy sauce, preferably, or 1 tablespoon plus 1 teaspoon regular soy sauce
1 tablespoon plus 1 teaspoon Dijon mustard
2 teaspoons brown sugar
¼ teaspoon ground allspice
2 tablespoons wasabi
Salt
Freshly ground pepper
3 tablespoons dry sherry
1 tablespoon gin

UTENSILS

Stockpot with cover
Large heavy-gauge skillet
Small saucepan
Large bowl
Small bowl
Saucer
18-inch jelly-roll pan
Platter
Chef's knife
Paring knife
Wooden spoon
Metal spatula
Vegetable peeler
Grater
Tongs
Nutcracker

START-TO-FINISH STEPS

1. Follow potatoes recipe steps 1 through 4.
2. Follow cabbage recipe steps 1 through 3.
3. Follow potatoes recipe steps 5 through 7.
4. Follow tempura sauce recipe steps 1 through 3 and sour cream sauce recipe steps 1 through 3.
5. Follow lobster recipe step 1 and citrus butter recipe step 1.
6. Follow lobster recipe step 2.
7. While lobsters are steaming, follow cabbage recipe step 4 and prepare wasabi sauce.
8. Follow citrus butter recipe step 2 and cabbage recipe step 5.
9. Follow lobster recipe step 3 and citrus butter recipe steps 3 and 4.
10. While completing citrus butter, follow potatoes recipe steps 8 and 9.
11. Follow lobster recipe step 4 and serve with cabbage and potatoes.

RECIPES

Steamed Lobster with Four Sauces

1½ teaspoons salt
4 live "chicken" lobsters (each about 1¼ pounds)
Sour cream sauce (see following recipe)
Spiced citrus butter (see following recipe)
Tempura sauce (see following recipe)
Wasabi sauce (see following recipe)

1. To stockpot large enough to hold all 4 lobsters without crowding, add enough water to come 5 or 6 inches up sides.

Add salt, cover pan, and bring to a boil over high heat.

2. With water at full rolling boil, plunge in lobsters, one at a time, head first, and cover pan. Adjust heat so that water simmers but does not boil. Cook 12 minutes from time last lobster goes in.

3. Remove pan from heat. With tongs, remove lobsters from water and drain. With chef's knife, slit shell on underbelly and crack lobster claws with nutcracker.

4. Place each lobster on a dinner plate and serve with the 4 sauces on the side.

Sour Cream Sauce

1 bunch fresh dill, or 1 tablespoon dried
1 teaspoon cider vinegar or rice vinegar
1 tablespoon plus 1 teaspoon Dijon mustard
½ cup sour cream
½ teaspoon salt
3 to 4 tablespoons milk

1. If using fresh dill, rinse and pat dry with paper towels. With chef's knife, mince enough leaves and tender stems to measure ⅔ cup, and place in small bowl. If using dried, sprinkle with vinegar and crush with fork to blend.

2. With fork, stir in vinegar, if it has not already been added, mustard, sour cream, and salt, stirring until blended. Slowly stir in enough milk to give sauce texture of heavy cream.

3. Turn into small ramekin, cover, and set aside.

Spiced Citrus Butter

1 lemon
Large juice orange
6 tablespoons salted butter
¼ teaspoon ground allspice
1 tablespoon gin

1. Wash lemon and orange, and pat dry with paper towels. On fine holes of grater, shred enough peel to measure 1 tablespoon lemon zest and 2 tablespoons orange zest. Halve lemon and orange. Squeeze enough lemon juice to measure 2 tablespoons, and enough orange juice to measure ¼ cup. Strain to remove pits.

2. In small saucepan used for potatoes, melt butter over medium heat. Add allspice and citrus zests, and cook, stirring occasionally, 4 to 5 minutes.

3. With wooden spoon, stir in juices and blend thoroughly. Raise heat to medium-high and bring sauce to a boil.

4. Let sauce bubble rapidly 2 to 3 minutes. Stir in gin, pour into small ramekin, and serve.

Tempura Sauce

Large clove garlic
1-inch piece fresh ginger (about ½ ounce)
2 teaspoons brown sugar
3 tablespoons dry sherry
2 tablespoons tamari or other aged soy sauce, preferably, or 1 tablespoon plus 1 teaspoon regular soy sauce

1. Peel garlic and ginger. On fine holes of grater, shred garlic, letting shreds fall into ramekin. You should have about 1 tablespoon. Shred ginger in same manner.

2. Add sugar, sherry, and tamari, stirring well after each addition until sugar is dissolved.

3. Cover, and set aside until ready to serve.

Wasabi Sauce

2 tablespoons wasabi

1. Place 2 tablespoons wasabi on saucer.

2. Slowly stir in water, a drop or two at a time, until sauce is texture of heavy cream. It will thicken as it stands.

3. Turn into small ramekin, cover loosely, and set aside.

Sautéed New Cabbage

Medium-size head green cabbage, preferably new crop (about 1½ pounds)
2 tablespoons salted butter
½ teaspoon salt

1. Remove coarse, limp outer leaves from cabbage.

2. Quarter cabbage and remove core. If core is tender and sweet, cut into ¼-inch dice; if tough, discard.

3. Using chef's knife or grater, shred cabbage as for slaw. Place shreds in large bowl and set aside.

4. In large heavy-gauge skillet, melt butter over medium heat. As soon as butter turns brown, add cabbage, a handful at a time. Raise heat to medium-high and cook, stirring frequently with wooden spoon, until cabbage is tender but still crisp, 8 to 10 minutes.

5. Stir in salt, reduce heat to very low, and keep warm.

Oven-Fried Potatoes

4 large baking potatoes (about 2½ pounds total weight)
1 tablespoon salted butter
⅓ cup vegetable oil
Salt

1. Preheat oven to 450 degrees.

2. In small saucepan, bring 3 cups water to a boil over high heat.

3. Peel potatoes and cut lengthwise into ⅓-inch-thick slabs. Cut slabs crosswise into ¾-inch-thick French fries. In jelly-roll pan, arrange potatoes in single layer.

4. Pull oven rack out slightly and place pan on it. Pour in enough boiling water to cover, about 2 cups. Carefully slide rack and pan into oven and bake 10 minutes.

5. Remove pan from oven and carefully pour off water.

6. Add butter and oil to potatoes and, with metal spatula, stir and toss until butter has melted and potatoes are coated evenly.

7. Return potatoes to oven and bake until crisp and well browned, about 35 to 40 minutes, stirring often with spatula and loosening any that stick to bottom of pan.

8. Transfer potatoes to paper-towel-lined platter and sprinkle generously with salt.

9. Turn potatoes into napkin-lined basket and serve.

Broiled Shark Steaks with Lime-Parsley Sauce
Rice with Walnuts
Broiled Vegetables

Choose large plates to accommodate the broiled fish steak, garnished with lime "wheels," the skewered broiled vegetables, and a serving of brown rice and walnuts. Serve any extra lime-parsley sauce in a small pitcher.

Shark meat—still a bargain—is a firm, dry, delicately flavored fish that many U.S. consumers overlook. The most popular varieties are the dark-fleshed mako and blue sharks. If you cannot find shark, use any other firm-fleshed fish like halibut or swordfish. Shark meat often has a mildly ammoniac taste; it requires brief soaking in a vinegar or citrus juice mixture to neutralize it.

Brown rice is unpolished white rice with its bran coating intact. The nutty flavor of the brown rice is complemented here by sautéed walnuts.

Let seasonal availability dictate your ingredient selection for the broiled vegetables. Instead of squash, the cook suggests substituting either red or green bell peppers, or long slender Japanese eggplant.

WHAT TO DRINK

Serve a soft wine with medium body and a touch of sweetness: a dry Chenin Blanc or French Colombard from California, or a dry Vouvray from France.

SHOPPING LIST AND STAPLES

4 shark, bluefin tuna, albacore, swordfish, or catfish steaks (each about 8 ounces)
Large yellow summer squash (about ¼ pound)
Large zucchini (about ¼ pound)
8 large mushrooms (4 to 5 ounces total weight)
Large bunch scallions
Small bunch chives (optional)
Large bunch parsley
Large clove garlic
2-inch piece fresh ginger
5 large limes plus 1 lime (optional)
1 pint sour cream
3 tablespoons salted butter
1 cup plus 1 tablespoon olive oil
2 tablespoons tamari, preferably, or other aged soy sauce
1 cup brown rice
4-ounce can walnut pieces
½ teaspoon ground cumin
Salt

UTENSILS

Food processor or blender
Small skillet with cover
2 small heavy-gauge saucepans, one with cover
2 large disposable foil broiling pans
Medium-size bowl
Small bowl
Measuring cups and spoons
Chef's knife
Paring knife
Wooden spoon
Grater
Juicer (optional)
Pastry brush
4 bamboo skewers

START-TO-FINISH STEPS

At least 30 minutes ahead: Soak bamboo skewers in water to prevent scorching.

1. Follow rice recipe step 1.
2. While rice is cooking, follow broiled vegetable recipe step 1. For shark recipe, mince parsley, slice ginger, squeeze lime juice, and, if using, cut lime "wheels" for garnish.
3. For rice recipe, grate lime zest, mince garlic, and mince scallion tops or snip chives for garnish, if using. Follow rice recipe step 2.
4. Follow shark recipe steps 1 and 2.
5. Follow rice recipe step 3.
6. Follow vegetables recipe step 2.
7. Follow rice recipe step 4 and vegetables recipe step 3.
8. Follow shark recipe step 3.
9. Follow vegetables recipe step 4 and rice recipe step 5.
10. Follow shark recipe steps 4 through 8 and vegetables recipe step 5.
11. Follow shark recipe step 9 and rice recipe step 6.
12. Follow shark recipe step 10, rice recipe step 7, and serve with vegetables.

RECIPES

Broiled Shark Steaks with Lime-Parsley Sauce

2 tablespoons tamari, preferably, or other aged soy sauce
½ teaspoon ground cumin
1 cup minced fresh parsley
½ cup lime juice
1 cup olive oil
2-inch piece fresh ginger, cut into ⅛-inch-thick slices

4 shark, bluefin tuna, albacore, swordfish, or catfish steaks (each about 8 ounces)
1⅓ cups sour cream
1 lime, thinly sliced into "wheels" for garnish (optional)

1. Preheat broiler and set broiler rack as close as possible to heating element.
2. For basting sauce, combine tamari, cumin, parsley, lime juice, olive oil, and ginger in small bowl. With fork, stir to combine. Set aside.
3. Wipe steaks with damp paper towels. Brush one side of each steak with oil that has risen to the top of reserved basting sauce, and arrange fish, oiled-sides down, in center of disposable broiling pan. Brush top sides with oil.
4. Broil fish 8 to 10 minutes. Do not turn. Fish is done when it flakes easily when tested with a fork and is opaque clear through.
5. Remove ginger from marinade and purée remainder of sauce in food processor or blender.
6. In small saucepan, bring sauce to a simmer over medium heat, stirring occasionally, 2 to 3 minutes.
7. Place sour cream in medium-size bowl and gradually add warmed sauce, stirring until blended.
8. Remove fish from broiler, cover loosely with aluminum foil, and keep warm on stove top.
9. Add pan juices to the sauce and stir to combine.
10. Divide steaks among 4 dinner plates and top each with a garnish of lime "wheels," if desired. Serve remaining sauce separately.

Rice with Walnuts

1 cup brown rice
½ teaspoon salt
3 tablespoons salted butter
Large clove garlic, minced
3 tablespoons grated lime zest (about 2 large limes)
1 cup coarsely broken walnuts
⅓ cup minced scallion tops or 3 tablespoons snipped chives for garnish (optional)

1. In small heavy-gauge saucepan, bring 2 cups water to a boil over high heat. Stir in rice and salt. Return to a boil, cover pan, reduce heat to low, and cook rice 40 minutes, or until all water is absorbed and rice is tender.
2. In small skillet, melt butter over medium heat. Add garlic and lime zest and sauté, stirring often, until garlic is golden and zest smells toasty, about 5 minutes.

3. Stir in walnuts and continue to sauté, stirring frequently with wooden spoon, until walnuts are golden brown, 5 to 8 minutes more.
4. Remove pan from heat and cover to keep warm until rice is done.
5. Remove rice from heat. Covered rice will keep at least 15 minutes.
6. Add walnut mixture to rice and, with fork, toss gently until combined.
7. Divide rice among 4 plates and garnish with chives or scallion tops, if desired.

Broiled Vegetables

Large yellow summer squash (about 1 pound)
Large zucchini (about ¼ pound)
Large bunch scallions
8 large mushrooms (4 to 5 ounces)
1 tablespoon olive oil, approximately

1. Rinse both squashes and pat dry with paper towels. With chef's knife, halve lengthwise and cut into 1-inch rounds. Trim scallions, leaving about 1 inch of the green, and cut into 2-inch lengths. Reserve green tops for rice recipe, if using for garnish. Wipe mushrooms with damp paper towels and halve.
2. Thread vegetables onto bamboo skewers, alternating scallions, mushrooms, zucchini, and summer squash. Skewer mushrooms through the cap, rather than through the stem, to prevent them from splitting.
3. Brush vegetables lightly with oil, place in disposable broiling pan, and broil about 2 minutes per side.
4. Remove vegetables from broiler, cover loosely with foil, and keep warm on stove top.
5. Uncover vegetables, return to broiler, and broil additional 2 minutes per side, or just until tender and lightly speckled with brown.

LEFTOVER SUGGESTION

Leftover rice and shark steak can be combined for a simple luncheon salad the following day. Flake the fish, then moisten it with any leftover sauce or with freshly squeezed lime juice. Add the fish to the cold rice and toss. To further enhance the salad, add cubes of ham, cooked and cooled shellfish, or any cut-up fresh or leftover cooked vegetables. Garnish the salad with walnuts or with croutons, if desired.

Lemon-Braised Celery, Endive, and Watercress
Haddock with Crab Meat and Hazelnut Stuffing

Garnish the stuffed haddock with lemon "wheels" and parsley sprigs. Serve the vegetables separately.

For the haddock entrée, ask the fish dealer to clean, bone, and butterfly the fish for you, leaving on its head and tail. Check the fish carefully for small bones as you eat it. If haddock is not available, use rock cod, sea bass, or any other mild, white-fleshed fish.

Look for hazelnuts, also known as filberts, in specialty food shops or health food stores. Toasting the hazelnuts is a simple process that brings out their delicate flavor fully. After the nuts cool, rub off their bitter skins, several nuts at a time, with a kitchen towel.

Currants, smaller, harder, and stronger-tasting than raisins, are a variety of tiny black grapes that are dried.

You may substitute chopped dark raisins, but their flavor and texture are different.

Whether you use fresh or frozen crab meat, carefully pick out any bits of shell or cartilage before adding the crab to the filling mixture.

Celery hearts, the cluster of inner ribs, should be crisp and have fresh-looking leaves. Endive and watercress, both slightly bitter greens, are good flavor foils for the bland celery. Slender, tapered heads of Belgian endive should be firm and crisp, with ivory leaves fringed in pale yellow. Much of the endive sold in this country is imported and is available in markets from autumn through spring.

Watercress should look fresh and bright green. Braising, an ideal way to cook the endive and the celery, both mellows and tenderizes them. The watercress, added during the last five minutes of cooking, retains its crisp texture and bright color.

The haddock is presented whole on a bed of extra filling. Carefully lift the fish from its baking pan with two spatulas so that it does not fall apart. Serve the fish and the vegetables on separate plates to prevent the mixing of the fish juices with the vegetable juices.

WHAT TO DRINK

Because of the richness of the haddock stuffing, a full-bodied wine is advisable. Choose a California Chardonnay or a white Burgundy, such as a Mâcon or St. Veran.

SHOPPING LIST AND STAPLES

1 whole haddock (4½ to 5 pounds), cleaned, boned, and butterflied, with head and tail left on
6 ounces cooked crabmeat, fresh or frozen
4 medium-size Belgian endives (1 to 1¼ pounds total weight)
2 bunches celery
Large bunch watercress
Large bunch parsley
1 lemon plus additional 2 lemons (optional)
Large clove garlic
4 shallots
5 tablespoons salted butter, approximately
1 egg
1 French baguette or long Italian bread
10-ounce package currants, preferably, or dark raisins
3 ounces hazelnuts
Salt
1 cup dry white wine

UTENSILS

Food processor or blender
Large non-aluminum skillet with cover
Small saucepan
Large roasting pan
Small heatproof baking dish
9-inch pie plate
Platter
Medium-size bowl
Small bowl
Colander
Salad spinner (optional)
Measuring cups and spoons
Chef's knife
Bread knife
Paring knife
Wooden spoon
2 metal spatulas
Wooden spatula
Rubber spatula
Juicer (optional)
Garlic press

START-TO-FINISH STEPS

1. Follow haddock recipe steps 1 and 2.
2. While hazelnuts are toasting, halve baguette (reserving other half for celery recipe), cut into 3 or 4 pieces, and, in food prcessor or blender, reduce to large crumbs. Follow haddock recipe step 3.
3. Wash parsley and pat dry with paper towels. Strip enough leaves from stems to measure ½ cup, reserving several sprigs for garnish, if desired. Chop raisins, if using. Follow haddock recipe steps 4 through 13.
4. Squeeze enough lemon to measure 1 tablespoon juice and follow celery recipe steps 1 through 3.
5. While endive and celery are cooking, slice remaining half of French bread and set aside. For haddock recipe, slice lemon "wheels" for garnish, if using.
6. Follow celery recipe step 4 and haddock recipe step 14, turning oven to broil as soon as you remove fish.
7. Follow celery recipe steps 5 and 6, haddock recipe steps 15 and 16, and serve.

RECIPES

Lemon-Braised Celery, Endive, and Watercress

2 bunches celery
4 medium-size Belgian endives (1 to 1¼ pounds total weight)
Large bunch watercress
Large clove garlic
2 tablespoons salted butter

1 tablespoon lemon juice
Twelve ½-inch slices French baguette or long Italian bread

1. Remove outer stalks of celery and keep for another use. Separate celery heart stalks, and trim bases. Rinse under cold water and pat dry with paper towels. Remove wilted outer leaves from endive. Pick over watercress, discarding any yellowed or wilted leaves as well as tough lower stems. In colander, rinse endive and watercress under cold running water and dry in salad spinner or pat dry with paper towels.
2. With chef's knife, cut celery into pieces 1½ inches long and ½ inch wide. Leave the leaves on the innermost stalks. Cut endive lengthwise into quarters. Peel garlic.
3. In skillet used for stuffing, melt butter over medium heat. With garlic press, crush garlic into skillet and cook, stirring with wooden spoon, 1 to 2 minutes. Add celery and endive, turning gently to coat with butter. Add lemon juice, reduce heat to medium-low, cover pan, and cook 5 to 6 minutes.
4. Uncover pan and gently stir in watercress. Raise heat to medium and, stirring frequently, continue to cook uncovered about 5 minutes, or until vegetables are crisp-tender.
5. Arrange bread slices on broiler rack and place in preheated broiler. Toast bread until golden, 1½ to 2 minutes per side. Transfer to napkin-lined basket.
6. Turn vegetables into serving dish and serve with toast on individual side dishes.

Haddock with Crab Meat and Hazelnut Stuffing

¾ cup hazelnuts
3 tablespoons salted butter, approximately
2½ cups coarse fresh bread crumbs
1 whole haddock (4½ to 5 pounds), cleaned, boned, and butterflied, with head and tail left on
6 ounces cooked crabmeat
4 shallots
½ cup parsley
½ teaspoon salt
1 tablespoon currants or chopped dark raisins
1 egg
1 cup dry white wine
Parsley sprigs for garnish (optional)
2 lemons, sliced into "wheels" for garnish (optional)

1. Preheat oven to 350 degrees.
2. In pie plate, arrange nuts in single layer. Toast 12 minutes, or until skins have split open and meat is light, golden brown. Remove from oven and allow to cool. Raise oven temperature to 375 degrees.
3. In large non-aluminum skillet, melt 2 tablespoons butter over medium heat. Add bread crumbs and fry, stirring occasionally with wooden spatula, until crumbs are golden brown. Remove pan from heat and set aside.
4. Rinse haddock inside and out under cold running water. With paper towels, wipe out bloodline from gut and pat fish dry.
5. In small bowl, pick over crabmeat, removing any shell or cartilage, and flake with fork. Set aside.
6. With paring knife, peel shallots. Using food processor or chef's knife, mince shallots and parsley. Transfer to medium-size bowl.
7. With kitchen towel, rub cooled hazelnuts to remove skins. A few brown spots will be left.
8. Turn hazelnuts into food processor and processs until nuts are same size as large bread crumbs. Or, using blender, process in small batches. With rubber spatula, scrape hazelnuts into bowl containing shallot-parsley mixture. Add fried bread crumbs, salt, currants, crab meat, and egg, and stir to combine thoroughly. Wipe out skillet.
9. Lightly butter large roasting pan.
10. In small saucepan, melt 1 tablespoon of butter over low heat.
11. Spread open body cavity of haddock and stuff it with as much of the crab meat-hazelnut mixture as will fit comfortably and still allow the flaps of the cavity to close around it completely. Wrap leftover stuffing in aluminum foil and place in small baking dish.
12. With your hands or using 2 metal spatulas, place fish in buttered roasting pan, drizzle with melted butter, and pour wine around, but not over, it.
13. Bake fish and foil-wrapped stuffing in upper third of preheated oven, 15 to 20 minutes, or until fish flakes easily when tested near the thick part of the backbone with tip of knife.
14. Remove fish and stuffing packet from oven. Raise temperature to broil for bread.
15. Open packet and form a bed of stuffing on serving platter large enough to hold fish. Using 2 spatulas, carefully lift fish out and place on stuffing.
16. Cover eyes with parsley sprigs and garnish platter with lemon "wheels" and parsley sprigs, if desired.

Paul Neuman and Stacy Bogdonoff

MENU 1 (Right)
Poached Salmon with Green Sauce
Rice Pilaf with Scallions
Asparagus with Lemon Glaze

MENU 2
Mediterranean Fish Stew
Basil Toasts
Watercress and Endive Salad
with Warm Olive Oil Dressing

MENU 3
Broiled Swordfish with Herb Butter
Sautéed Spinach with Shallots
New Potatoes Braised in Broth with Leeks

Though Paul Neuman never trained as a cook, he has had extensive experience in the food business, including work at his family's Manhattan fish market. He and Stacy Bogdonoff, his wife, now run a Manhattan catering service. He believes that food preparation must be simple and direct. Most importantly, meals must be aesthetically appealing, with vivid, often contrasting, colors and textures—a concept he derived from Japanese cuisine.

With classical training in French cooking, Stacy Bogdonoff brings to this team the technical competence to produce *haute cuisine*. Nevertheless, she describes herself as an untraditional cook who, like her husband, prefers vivid, visual foods.

As they cook and plan menus together, they select a central element or ingredient, something they like to cook, and build the meal around that. They always follow a cardinal rule: Plan a meal for flavor and visual impact. The themes for Menu 1 and Menu 3 are similar: Pale-fleshed fish steaks—salmon and swordfish—play off the bright greens of the vegetables and the pale greens of the fish sauces.

The dramatic fish chowder of Menu 2 is richly textured and colorful. Served in a shallow bowl, the mussel shells and chunks of seafood are half-covered with the orange-red liquid. The endive and watercress salad and the basil toast create additional textures and colors.

When you serve this elegant spring or summer meal, arrange the salmon steaks on a platter with the warm green sauce, and garnish with watercress sprigs. Pass the asparagus spears and the rice pilaf in separate dishes. If you have them, use white serving pieces to emphasize the various shades of green and white in this meal.

Poached Salmon with Green Sauce
Rice Pilaf with Scallions
Asparagus with Lemon Glaze

In this menu the main-course fish is cooked by poaching, a low-calorie cooking method that uses no fat. The barely simmering poaching liquid can contain many seasonings or may be flavored only with lemon juice, as in this recipe. It must never boil because the rapid water movement would break the fish apart, marring both flavor and appearance. Firm-fleshed fish such as salmon (or its substitutes in this recipe, sea bass or striped bass) are best for poaching. Save half a cup of poaching liquid for the accompanying sauce, and store the rest in the refrigerator or freezer for future use. The green sauce calls for fresh dill, but you can substitute parsley or basil.

Select plump, bright-green asparagus with compact tips. Before storing the spears, cut a small piece from the bottom of each, then stand them upright in a container of cold water in the refrigerator. If fresh asparagus are not available, use any green vegetable in season—perhaps broccoli, green beans, or snow peas.

WHAT TO DRINK

To complement the delicate salmon and sauce, choose a subtle wine such as a Riesling.

SHOPPING LIST AND STAPLES

4 center-cut fillets of salmon, sea bass, or striped bass, or 1-inch-thick steaks (each about 8 ounces)
16 asparagus spears (about 1 pound total weight), or 1 pound green beans, broccoli, or snow peas
2 stalks celery
Large yellow onion
2 shallots
4 large lemons
Medium-size bunch watercress
Medium-size bunch scallions
Medium-size bunch parsley
Medium-size bunch chives
Small bunch dill
1 stick plus 2 tablespoons unsalted butter
½ pint heavy cream
1½ cups chicken stock, preferably homemade (see page 13), or canned (optional)
¾ cup long-grain white rice
3 tablespoons vegetable oil
1 tablespoon Dijon mustard
Salt

Freshly ground white pepper
Freshly ground black pepper
3 tablespoons dry white wine
3 tablespoons sweet vermouth

UTENSILS

Food processor or blender
3 large skillets, one with cover
1 small saucepan
2 small enamel-lined saucepans, one with cover
2 heatproof serving platters
Heatproof plate
Serving bowl
Colander
Salad spinner (optional)
Measuring cups and spoons
Chef's knife
Paring knife
1 or 2 slotted spatulas
Wooden spatula
Rubber spatula
Whisk
Vegetable peeler
Colander

START-TO-FINISH STEPS

1. Follow pilaf recipe steps 1 and 2.
2. While vegetables are cooking, follow green sauce recipe steps 1 and 2 and salmon recipe step 1.
3. Follow green sauce recipe step 3.
4. While cream is reducing, follow pilaf recipe steps 3 and 4.
5. While stock is coming to a boil, follow salmon recipe steps 2 and 3.
6. Juice lemons for salmon and asparagus recipes. Follow salmon recipe step 4 and pilaf recipe step 5.
7. While pilaf is cooking, follow asparagus recipe steps 1 and 2.
8. Follow salmon recipe step 5 and green sauce recipe step 4.
9. While sauce is reducing, place serving platters for salmon and asparagus and bowl for pilaf in oven to warm and follow asparagus recipe step 3.
10. Follow green sauce recipe step 5 and asparagus recipe step 4.

11. Follow green sauce recipe step 6.

12. Follow asparagus recipe step 5, green sauce recipe step 7, pilaf recipe step 6, salmon recipe step 6, and serve.

RECIPES

Poached Salmon with Green Sauce

4 center-cut fillets of salmon, sea bass, or striped bass, or 1-inch-thick steaks (each about 8 ounces),
½ cup lemon juice
Green sauce (see following recipe)
8 sprigs of watercress (optional)

1. Wipe salmon with damp paper towels.

2. In each of 2 large skillets, bring 2 inches water and ¼ cup lemon juice to a boil over high heat. Reduce to a simmer.

3. Preheat oven to 200 degrees.

4. Add salmon in single layer, making sure fish is completely covered by liquid (add more water if necessary). Return water to a simmer and poach salmon, being careful not to boil, until fish turns light pink all the way through, 8 to 10 minutes. Using sharp stainless steel knife, make a small slit in center of salmon to check color.

5. With 1 or 2 slotted spatulas, transfer fish to heatproof plate and keep warm in preheated oven. Measure ½ cup poaching liquid and reserve for sauce. Discard remaining liquid. Rinse out 1 skillet.

6. Pour small amount of sauce on heated serving platter, top with salmon, and cover with remaining sauce. Garnish with sprigs of watercress, if desired.

Green Sauce

2 shallots
½ medium-size bunch watercress
Small bunch dill
1 cup heavy cream
3 tablespoons dry white wine
3 tablespoons sweet vermouth
½ cup reserved salmon poaching liquid
Salt and freshly ground black pepper
2 tablespoons unsalted butter

1. Wash, peel, and finely mince shallots. Set aside.

2. In colander, wash watercress and dill. Dry in salad spinner or pat dry with paper towels. Remove stems and discard. In food processor or blender, combine watercress and dill, and process until smooth. Set aside.

3. In small saucepan, reduce cream by half over medium-high heat, about 10 to 15 minutes.

4. In small enamel-lined saucepan, combine wine, vermouth, poaching liquid, and shallots. Bring to a boil over medium-high heat, and cook until liquid is reduced by half, about 8 to 10 minutes.

5. Reduce heat to medium. Add reduced cream to wine mixture, whisking until blended, and cook just until sauce thickens, about 3 to 5 minutes.

6. With rubber spatula, scrape processed watercress and dill into sauce. Add salt and pepper to taste, and whisk until blended.

7. Remove pan from heat and add 1 tablespoon butter at a time, whisking until totally incorporated.

Rice Pilaf with Scallions

2 stalks celery
Medium-size bunch scallions
Large yellow onion
3 tablespoons vegetable oil
¾ cup long-grain white rice
1½ cups chicken stock or water
Salt and freshly ground white pepper
½ cup chopped parsley

1. Wash celery and scallions, and pat dry with paper towels. With chef's knife, trim off ends of celery and scallions and finely dice. Peel and dice onion.

2. In large skillet, heat oil over medium heat. Add celery and onion, and sauté, stirring frequently with wooden spatula, until vegetables are translucent, about 10 minutes.

3. Add scallions and rice, and sauté, stirring, another 3 to 5 minutes.

4. Add stock or water, stir, and bring to a boil over high heat.

5. Cover, reduce heat to medium, and cook until rice is tender and has absorbed liquid, about 18 minutes. Remove pan from heat and keep covered until ready to serve.

6. Fluff rice with fork and season with salt and white pepper to taste. Turn into warmed serving bowl and sprinkle with parsley.

Asparagus with Lemon Glaze

16 spears fresh asparagus (about 1 pound total weight), or 1 pound green beans, broccoli, or snow peas
1 stick unsalted butter
⅓ cup lemon juice
Medium-size bunch chives
1 tablespoon Dijon mustard
Salt and freshly ground black pepper

1. Wash asparagus and break off ends. Peel stems and, if necessary, trim ends to make spears of uniform length. Set aside. Wash, pat dry, and mince ⅓ cup plus 1 teaspoon chives.

2. In small enamel-lined saucepan melt butter over low heat. Add lemon juice, ⅓ cup chives, mustard, and salt and pepper to taste. Cover partially and keep warm over very low heat.

3. In large skillet used for salmon, bring 2 inches water to a boil over high heat.

4. Place asparagus in skillet, return water to a boil, and cook spears 4 to 5 minutes, until bright green and tender but still firm.

5. Drain asparagus in colander and place on warmed serving platter. Pour lemon butter over asparagus and garnish with remaining chives.

Mediterranean Fish Stew
Basil Toasts
Watercress and Endive Salad with Warm Olive Oil Dressing

The richly seasoned Mediterranean chowder contains vegetables, herbs, and four varieties of seafood. The mackerel for the chowder is either king mackerel, an oily, strong-flavored fish, or Spanish mackerel, leaner and more delicately flavored. If neither is available fresh, use frozen, but not canned. When buying live mussels, check that their shells are tightly closed. For any with open shells, test if they are alive by trying to slide the two shells laterally across one another. Discard any with shells that move or that remain open and also discard any mussels

Garnish the appetizingly colorful Mediterranean fish stew with chopped parsley. To accompany this substantial entrée, pass crisp basil toasts and a salad of watercress and endive. Informal serving pieces are ideal.

that do not open during cooking. Raw shrimp should be firm and odor free. See page 11 for shelling and deveining instructions.

Since squid is usually sold whole, ask the fish dealer to clean it and cut it up. Otherwise, follow the directions on pages 11–12.

Fresh fennel and saffron threads flavor the chowder base. Fennel has a delicate anise flavor; it is available in Italian groceries and some supermarkets. If fresh fennel is unavailable, use fennel seeds and four stalks of sliced celery. Grind saffron threads with a mortar and pestle or pulverize them with your fingers between two sheets of wax paper.

Basil toasts can be prepared up to five days in advance and stored in an air-tight container.

WHAT TO DRINK

Mediterranean flavors go with Mediterranean wines. Serve a French rosé, such as a Lirac or a Tavel, or a full-bodied Italian white, such as a Greco di Tufo.

SHOPPING LIST AND STAPLES

12 mussels
1 pound whole king or Spanish mackerel, boned
½ pound medium-size fresh shrimp
2 squid (about 1 pound total weight), cleaned and cut into rings
1 fennel bulb, or 1 tablespoon fennel seeds
2 large yellow onions
6 cloves garlic
2 or 3 shallots
2 bunches watercress
2 heads endive
Small bunch parsley
Small bunch fresh basil, or 3 teaspoons dried
1 orange
1 lemon
1 egg
1 stick unsalted butter
¼ pound Parmesan cheese
32-ounce can Italian plum tomatoes
6-ounce can tomato paste
¾ cup plus 2 tablespoons olive oil
¼ cup walnut oil
¼ cup sherry vinegar or balsamic vinegar
1 teaspoon saffron threads
1 long loaf crusty French bread
Salt and freshly ground pepper
½ cup white Burgundy wine

UTENSILS

Small skillet
Large heavy-gauge enamel or stainless steel saucepan or stockpot with cover
Small saucepan
17 x 11-inch cookie sheet
Salad bowl
Small bowl
Salad spinner (optional)
Measuring cups and spoons
Chef's knife
Serrated knife
Paring knife
Wooden spoon
Metal spatula

Wooden spatula
Ladle
Grater
Whisk
Pastry brush
Mortar and pestle (optional)
Stiff scrubbing brush

START-TO-FINISH STEPS

1. Follow fish stew recipe steps 1 through 3.
2. While onions are sautéing, wash, dry, and chop basil for fish stew and basil toasts recipes. Grate Parmesan for basil toasts recipe.
3. Follow fish stew recipe step 4.
4. While tomato mixture is cooking, follow fish stew recipe step 5, basil toasts recipe steps 1 through 4, and salad recipe steps 1 through 3.
5. Follow basil toasts recipe step 5 and fish stew recipe step 6.
6. While fish is cooking, follow salad recipe steps 4 and 5.
7. Warm serving bowl and platter under hot running water. Dry. Follow fish stew recipe step 7, salad recipe step 6, and serve with basil toasts.

RECIPES

Mediterranean Fish Stew

2 large yellow onions
6 cloves garlic
1 fennel bulb, or 1 tablespoon fennel seeds
1 teaspoon saffron threads
6 tablespoons olive oil
½ cup white Burgundy wine
32-ounce can Italian plum tomatoes
¼ cup tomato paste
1 tablespoon chopped fresh basil, or 1 teaspoon dried
12 mussels
½ pound medium-size fresh shrimp
1 pound whole king or Spanish mackerel, boned
1 orange
2 squid (about 1 pound total weight), cleaned and cut into rings
2 tablespoons chopped fresh parsley for garnish (optional)

1. With chef's knife, peel and slice onions, and peel and chop garlic. Wash and slice fennel bulb, if using.
2. Using mortar and pestle or with fingers, crush saffron.
3. In large heavy-gauge saucepan or stockpot, heat oil over medium-high heat until hot but not smoking. Add onions and fresh fennel, if using. Sauté, stirring with wooden spoon, until onions are soft but not transparent, about 5 minutes. Add garlic, saffron, and wine. Cook 1 minute.
4. Add tomatoes, tomato paste, basil, and fennel seed, if using. Break up tomatoes with spoon. Cover, reduce heat to low, and cook 30 to 35 minutes.

5. With stiff brush, scrub mussels under cold running water. Pull off any beards. Shell and devein shrimp. Cut mackerel into 1½-inch pieces. Finely grate enough orange rind to measure 2 tablespoons.
6. Stir in orange rind. Add mussels to tomato mixture and cook 2 minutes. Add shrimp and squid, then gently top with fish pieces. Cook 3 minutes. Turn off heat.
7. When ready to serve, gently ladle stew into serving bowl, so that fish pieces do not fall apart. If desired, garnish with chopped parsley.

Basil Toasts

¼ cup freshly grated Parmesan cheese
2 or 3 shallots
1 long loaf crusty French bread
1 stick unsalted butter
2 tablespoons finely chopped fresh basil, or 2 teaspoons dried

1. Preheat oven to 425 degrees.
2. With chef's knife, peel shallots and mince finely.
3. With serrated knife, cut bread into ¾-inch-thick slices and arrange in single layer on cookie sheet.
4. In small skillet, melt butter over low heat. Add shallots and sauté, stirring with wooden spatula, until just translucent, about 3 minutes. Add basil and stir to blend.
5. Brush bread slices with herb butter and sprinkle with cheese. Bake until lightly browned, 8 to 10 minutes.

Watercress and Endive Salad with Warm Olive Oil Dressing

2 bunches watercress
2 heads endive
1 lemon
½ cup olive oil
¼ cup walnut oil
¼ cup sherry vinegar or balsamic vinegar
1 egg
Salt
Freshly ground pepper

1. Wash watercress and remove stems. Dry in salad spinner or pat dry with paper towels.
2. Remove bruised outer leaves of endive. With chef's knife, cut endive into ¼-inch-thick diagonal slices, from tip to root end.
3. In salad bowl, combine watercress and endive. Cover and place in refrigerator. Squeeze enough lemon juice to measure 2 teaspoons.
4. In small saucepan, heat olive oil and walnut oil over medium heat just until warm. Off heat, add vinegar and lemon juice. Remove pits, if necessary.
5. In small bowl, separate egg, retaining yolk and discarding white. In a slow, steady stream, add oil and vinegar mixture, whisking constantly until sauce is smooth and thick. Season with salt and pepper to taste.
6. Remove greens from refrigerator, toss with dressing, and serve.

Broiled Swordfish with Herb Butter
Sautéed Spinach with Shallots
New Potatoes Braised in Broth with Leeks

Sautéed spinach with a twist of orange rind, together with new potatoes braised with leeks, provide appealing color contrasts to the swordfish steaks, which are capped with medallions of herb butter.

Swordfish has firm flesh and a flavor that can stand alone without elaborate sauces or seasonings. An uncomplicated herb butter is, in fact, the ideal sauce. Make the butter in advance, if you prefer, and store it, for up to 3 days in the refrigerator or up to 6 weeks in the freezer, rolled in a log shape and wrapped in wax paper. To serve, slice rounds from the roll and place on top of the fish steaks just before serving.

The sautéed spinach dish calls for shallots, considered the aristocrat of onions because of their very delicate flavor. The spinach is tossed with a medley of citrus juices—lemon, orange, and lime—which add a subtle flavor to the dish.

Buy straight, slender leeks, avoiding those that have become bulbous, as they may be woody and flavorless. Choose those with the greenest tops and wash them thoroughly. Coarse mustard, an essential flavoring ingredient in the stock, contains crushed mustard seeds, unlike Dijon mustards. Imported and domestic coarse mustards are sold in most supermarkets.

WHAT TO DRINK

These dishes are simple and direct, and the wine should match them; choose a California Pinot Blanc, a dry Vouvray from the Loire, or a white Burgundy.

SHOPPING LIST AND STAPLES

Four 1-inch-thick swordfish steaks (each about 8 ounces)
1½ to 2 pounds young spinach
1½ pounds new red potatoes
Medium-size leek
2 shallots
1 clove garlic
¼ cup mixed fresh herbs, such as watercress, parsley, dill, basil, marjoram, and rosemary, or 2 tablespoons dried
2 lemons
1 lime
1 orange
2 sticks unsalted butter
1 to 1¼ cups chicken stock, preferably homemade (see page 13), or canned
¼ cup olive oil
2 tablespoons coarse mustard
Salt

Freshly ground white pepper
Freshly ground black pepper
½ cup dry white wine

UTENSILS

Food processor or blender (optional)
2 large skillets, one with cover
Medium-size skillet
Broiler pan
Medium-size bowl, plus one additional if not using food processor
Small bowl
Measuring cups and spoons
Chef's knife
Paring knife
Wooden spoon
Slotted spoon
Metal spatula
Rubber spatula
Wooden spatula
Juicer (optional)
Pastry brush

START-TO-FINISH STEPS

At least 1 hour ahead: Follow herb butter recipe steps 1 through 3.

1. Follow spinach recipe steps 1 and 2.
2. Follow potatoes recipe steps 1 through 5.
3. Follow swordfish recipe steps 1 and 2.
4. Follow potatoes recipe step 6 and swordfish recipe step 3. Warm plates under hot running water.
5. Follow swordfish recipe step 4, potatoes recipe step 7, and spinach recipe steps 3 through 5.
6. Follow swordfish recipe step 5. While steaks finish broiling, dry plates.
7. Follow swordfish recipe step 6, potato recipe step 8, and spinach recipe step 6 and serve.

RECIPES

Broiled Swordfish with Herb Butter

Four 1-inch-thick swordfish steaks (each about 8 ounces)
¼ cup olive oil
Herb butter (see following recipe)

1. Preheat broiler. Place broiler pan 3 to 4 inches from heating element and heat 3 to 5 minutes.
2. Wipe swordfish with damp paper towels. Lightly brush both sides of steaks with oil.
3. Place steaks on broiler pan and broil 4 to 5 minutes.
4. Using metal spatula, turn steaks and broil 2 to 3 minutes longer.
5. Cut 1 or 2 generous slices herb butter for each steak. Top steaks with butter and broil 1 minute longer, or just until butter begins to melt.
6. Transfer steaks to warm plates.

Herb Butter

1 stick unsalted butter, at room temperature
1 clove garlic
½ lemon
½ lime
¼ cup mixed fresh herbs (any combination, including watercress, parsley, dill, basil, marjoram, and rosemary), or 2 tablespoons dried

1. Peel and finely chop garlic. Juice enough lemon to measure 2 tablespoons and enough lime to measure 1 tablespoon. Combine juices and remove pits. Wash fresh herbs, if using, pat dry, and chop finely.
2. In food processor or blender, combine butter, garlic, citrus juices, and chopped herbs, and process until well mixed. Or, in medium-size bowl, knead same ingredients together by hand.
3. Form herb butter into log-shaped roll 2 inches long and 2 to 2½ inches in diameter. Wrap snugly in wax paper and place in freezer for 1 hour or refrigerate for several hours.

Sautéed Spinach with Shallots

1½ to 2 pounds young spinach
2 shallots
4 tablespoons unsalted butter
1 lemon
½ orange
½ lime
Salt
Freshly ground white pepper
4 orange twists (optional)

1. Wash spinach thoroughly, remove stems, and place wet leaves in medium-size bowl. Peel shallots and chop enough to measure 2 tablespoons.

2. Squeeze ¼ cup lemon juice, 3 to 4 tablespoons orange juice, and 1 tablespoon lime juice. In small bowl, combine juices and remove pits.
3. In large skillet heat butter over medium-high heat until foamy. Add shallots and toss lightly with wooden spatula for 1 minute, removing skillet from heat to keep shallots from burning if necessary.
4. Add spinach and toss to combine thoroughly with butter and shallots.
5. While spinach is still bright green, push to one side of skillet and pour citrus juices into pan. Reduce juices over medium-high heat 30 seconds, then quickly toss spinach with juices and salt and pepper to taste.
6. Serve alongside swordfish steaks and, if desired, garnish each serving with an orange twist.

New Potatoes Braised in Broth with Leeks

1½ pounds new red potatoes
1 to 1¼ cups chicken stock
½ cup dry white wine
2 tablespoons coarse mustard
Medium-size leek
4 tablespoons unsalted butter
Salt
Freshly ground pepper

1. Wash potatoes but do not peel. Cut into quarters.
2. In large skillet, combine stock, wine, and mustard. Bring to a boil over medium-high heat, then reduce to a simmer.
3. Trim off root ends and upper leaves of leek, leaving some green, and split leek lengthwise. Gently spread leaves and rinse under cold running water, to remove any sand and grit. Pat dry with paper towel. With chef's knife, cut into ¼-inch slices.
4. Add potatoes to simmering broth. Cover and simmer 5 to 7 minutes.
5. In medium-size skillet melt butter over medium-low heat. Add leek and, stirring with wooden spoon, sauté 8 to 10 minutes.
6. Remove cover from potatoes and simmer uncovered 4 to 5 minutes.
7. Add leeks to potatoes, using rubber spatula to scrape out butter. Cook uncovered 5 minutes, turning occasionally, until broth is reduced and buttery leeks glaze the potatoes. Sprinkle with salt and pepper to taste.
8. With slotted spoon, transfer to dinner plates.

Patricia Unterman

MENU 1 (Left)
**Avocado and Grapefruit Salad
with Walnut Oil Dressing
Creole Fish and Oyster Stew
Baked Rice with Almonds**

MENU 2
**Fish Baked in Parchment with Red Peppers
Polenta with Butter and Cheese
Marinated Salad**

MENU 3
**Fresh Tomato and Fennel Soup
Trout Baked in Coarse Salt
Chard in Butter and Garlic
New Potatoes with Basil**

Californian Patricia Unterman comes from a family that loves to cook and to eat. Her mother taught her that food should be simple and the basic ingredients of the highest quality. At the San Francisco restaurant that she owns and runs with a partner, Patricia Unterman bases all her cooking on these two principles: "My partner and I founded the restaurant on the premise that the freshest ingredients need minimal preparation to improve them," she says.

She favors unusual varieties of fresh fish, which she most often grills over a mesquite wood fire and serves with a quickly made sauce; her recipes are flexible, so that a home cook can substitute whatever fish is freshest. She suggests several alternate choices in each menu.

She deals with vegetables in the same spirit, selecting the freshest and seasoning them lightly, as with the Swiss chard with butter and garlic, and the new potatoes with olive oil and basil of Menu 3. Menu 1 and Menu 2 feature salads tossed with delicately flavored vinaigrettes.

This informal meal features a Creole fish and oyster stew served in large soup bowls. Serve the almond-studded rice separately. Carefully arrange the avocado and grapefruit sections on a bed of watercress and lettuce leaves.

Avocado and Grapefruit Salad with Walnut Oil Dressing
Creole Fish and Oyster Stew
Baked Rice with Almonds

Many varieties of fish will combine well for this spicy stew. If you are using a firm-textured fish like swordfish, pompano, cod, or salmon, add it to the stew earlier than you would a more delicate fish, such as sole or halibut, for longer cooking. Oysters should always go in last, and simmer just until their edges begin to curl.

If you decide to use the optional fresh jalapeño pepper—a small fiery Mexican chili—sample it first for hotness: Slice it in half and taste a piece of it. If it is very hot, use just half of the pepper. However, if you like red-hot food, use the whole pepper, finely minced.

WHAT TO DRINK

This menu demands a wine with enough body to accompany the fish and enough flavor not to disappear in the face of the spices. A California or Alsatian Gewürztraminer will fill the bill.

SHOPPING LIST AND STAPLES

1 pound salmon fillets (if available)
1 pound fillets of halibut, petrale sole, pompano,
   swordfish, or cod, plus 1 additional pound
   if not using salmon
12 to 16 shucked oysters with liquor
2 medium-size ripe avocados
Medium-size red bell pepper
Medium-size onion
7 shallots
2 cloves garlic
1 bunch celery
1 head red-leaf lettuce
Large bunch watercress
Small bunch fresh oregano, or ¾ teaspoon dried
1 fresh jalapeño or serrano chili pepper (optional)
2 grapefruits (yellow or pink)
1 pint half-and-half
1 stick unsalted butter
1 cup fish stock, preferably homemade (see page 13),
   or 8-ounce bottle clam juice
¼ cup walnut oil
¼ cup sherry vinegar
1 cup long-grain white rice
3½-ounce package slivered almonds
¾ teaspoon paprika
½ teaspoon curry powder

¼ teaspoon cumin
Cayenne pepper
Salt
Freshly ground white pepper
Freshly ground black pepper

UTENSILS

Medium-size flameproof casserole with cover
Large heavy-gauge skillet
Medium-size saucepan with cover
Medium-size bowl
Small bowl
Salad bowl
Salad spinner (optional)
Measuring cups and spoons
Chef's knife
Paring knife
Ladle
Wooden spatula
Wooden spoon
Whisk
Thin rubber gloves (if using chili pepper)

START-TO-FINISH STEPS

1. Follow salad recipe steps 1 through 5.
2. Follow fish stew recipe steps 1 and 2.
3. Follow rice recipe steps 1 through 3.
4. Follow fish stew recipe steps 3 through 6.
5. Follow rice recipe steps 4 and 5.
6. While rice is cooking, follow salad recipe step 6 and serve.
7. Follow fish stew recipe steps 7 and 8, and serve with rice.

RECIPES

Avocado and Grapefruit Salad with Walnut Oil Dressing

2 grapefruits (yellow or pink)
2 medium-size ripe avocados
1 shallot
Large bunch watercress
1 head red-leaf lettuce
¼ cup sherry vinegar

½ teaspoon salt
Freshly ground black pepper
¼ cup walnut oil

1. With paring knife, peel grapefruit, removing all the white pith. Holding the peeled grapefruit over medium-size bowl to catch juice, cut between section membranes and let sections fall into bowl. Squeeze remaining membranes to remove any juice. Discard membranes.
2. With paring knife, peel avocados and cut in half lengthwise. Twist halves apart and remove pit. Slice halves lengthwise and add to bowl. With wooden spoon, toss very gently to coat with juice.
3. With chef's knife, peel shallot and chop finely. Trim watercress stems. Remove outer leaves from lettuce and reserve for another use.
4. Wash watercress and lettuce, and dry in salad spinner or pat dry with paper towels. Place in salad bowl, cover, and refrigerate.
5. In small bowl, combine shallot, vinegar, and salt and pepper to taste. Add half of juice from bowl with grapefruit and avocados. In a slow, steady stream, add walnut oil, whisking vigorously until combined.
6. Remove salad bowl from refrigerator. Add half of dressing to watercress and lettuce, and toss until greens are lightly coated. Taste for seasoning. Arrange alternating slices of avocado and grapefruit on top of greens and drizzle with remaining dressing.

Creole Fish and Oyster Stew

Medium-size red bell pepper
Medium-size green bell pepper
6 shallots
2 cloves garlic
2 inner stalks celery
1½ teaspoons fresh oregano, or ¾ teaspoon dried
1 fresh jalapeño or serrano chili pepper (optional)
6 tablespoons unsalted butter
1½ cups half-and-half
1 cup fish stock or clam juice
¾ teaspoon paprika
½ teaspoon curry powder
¼ teaspoon cumin
½ teaspoon salt
¼ teaspoon freshly ground white pepper
Cayenne pepper
1 pound salmon fillet (if available)

1 pound of fillets of halibut, petrale sole, pompano, swordfish, or cod, plus 1 additional pound if not using salmon
12 to 16 shucked oysters with liquor

1. Rinse bell peppers, pat dry with paper towels, core, and seed. Peel shallots and garlic. Wash and trim celery.
2. With chef's knife, mince garlic and finely chop bell peppers, shallots, and celery. Set aside. Wash, dry, and chop fresh oregano, if using. Wearing thin rubber gloves, rinse and seed chili pepper, if using. Finely chop and set aside.
3. In large heavy-gauge skillet melt butter over medium heat. Add bell peppers, shallots, and celery, and sauté until tender, 8 to 10 minutes.
4. Add garlic and oregano to skillet, and cook 30 seconds.
5. Add half-and-half and fish stock or clam juice and bring to a simmer over medium-high heat. Add chili pepper, if using, and paprika, curry powder, cumin, salt, white pepper, and Cayenne to taste, stirring to combine.
6. While fish stock is simmering, wipe fish fillets with damp paper towels. With chef's knife, cut fish into 1-inch pieces.
7. Add fish to skillet, adding halibut and petrale sole if using, after 1 minute. Return liquid to a simmer, and simmer just until fish is firm, 4 to 5 minutes.
8. Add oysters and liquor, and simmer just until edges of oysters start to curl, about 30 seconds. Check seasoning and ladle into individual soup bowls.

Baked Rice with Almonds

1 teaspoon salt
½ medium-size onion
2 tablespoons unsalted butter
½ cup slivered almonds
1 cup long-grain white rice

1. Preheat oven to 375 degrees.
2. In medium-size covered saucepan, bring 2 cups water and salt to a boil over high heat.
3. With chef's knife, peel and finely chop onion.
4. In flameproof casserole, melt butter over medium heat. Add onion and almonds, and sauté, stirring with wooden spatula, until onion is translucent and almonds are lightly browned, 3 to 5 minutes.
5. Add rice and stir until coated with butter. Pour in boiling water, stir, and bake, covered, until rice has absorbed all water and is tender but still firm, about 18 minutes.

Fish Baked in Parchment with Red Peppers
Polenta with Butter and Cheese
Marinated Salad

Fish baked in parchment with julienned red peppers is the focal point of this light meal. Garnish each serving of polenta with a sprig of watercress. The marinated salad, arranged on lettuce leaves, is served on individual plates.

Baking fish in kitchen parchment seals in the fish juices and gently steeps the fish in herbs and seasonings to create a flavorful sauce. If you cannot find parchment, substitute aluminum foil.

Polenta, or cornmeal mush, is a staple in northern Italy. This version calls for you to cook the polenta in a double boiler, stirring it frequently. It will become very stiff, so that when you turn the mixture onto a buttered board and flatten it, it will cool and harden enough to slice.

The marinated salad can accommodate any number of seasonal vegetables, but the mushrooms and black beans should be constant ingredients. As possible alternatives to the cucumbers, Patricia Unterman suggests blanched zucchini or cooked artichoke hearts. The balsamic vinegar in the dressing is a slightly sweet Italian red wine vinegar that is aged in barrels. If you cannot find it, substitute a good-quality red wine vinegar.

WHAT TO DRINK

An Italian wine is the best choice—either a crisp Verdicchio or the softer, fruitier Italian Chardonnay.

SHOPPING LIST AND STAPLES

Four 1-inch-thick fillets of tuna, halibut, sea bass, salmon, or haddock (each about 8 ounces)
½ pound mushrooms
½ pound broccoli
1 pint cherry tomatoes
4 red bell peppers (about 1¼ pounds total weight)
Medium-size cucumber
1 head Boston lettuce
Small bunch watercress (optional)
Medium-size red onion
Small onion
4 cloves garlic
1 fresh jalapeño or serrano chili pepper (optional)
1 tablespoon chopped fresh oregano, or 1 teaspoon dried
1 stick plus 2 tablespoons unsalted butter, approximately
¼ pound Parmesan cheese
¾ cup virgin olive oil
¼ cup balsamic vinegar
1 cup yellow cornmeal
¼ pound dried black beans
Salt and freshly ground pepper

UTENSILS

Medium-size skillet
Large saucepan
Medium-size saucepan
Small saucepan
Double boiler
Cookie sheet
Large bowl
Medium-size bowl
Small bowl
Colander

Salad spinner (optional)
Measuring cups and spoons
Chef's knife
Paring knife
2 wooden spoons
Metal spatula
Wooden spatula
Grater
Whisk
Vegetable peeler
Four 12 x 16-inch pieces baking parchment (optional)
Thin rubber gloves

START-TO-FINISH STEPS

1. Follow salad recipe step 1.
2. While beans are cooking, follow polenta recipe steps 1 through 5.
3. While polenta is cooking, follow salad recipe steps 2 through 8.
4. Follow fish recipe steps 1 through 9.
5. While fish is baking, follow salad recipe steps 9 through 11.
6. Follow polenta recipe steps 6 through 8.
7. Follow fish recipe steps 10 and 11, polenta recipe step 9, and serve with marinated salad.

RECIPES

Fish Baked in Parchment with Red Peppers

Four 1-inch thick fillets of tuna, halibut, sea bass, salmon, or haddock (each about 8 ounces)
4 red bell peppers (about 1¼ pounds total weight)
¼ cup virgin olive oil
4 cloves garlic
1 tablespoon chopped fresh oregano, or 1 teaspoon dried
Salt and freshly ground pepper
Medium-size red onion
1 fresh jalapeño or serrano chili pepper (optional)
2 tablespoons unsalted butter

1. With damp paper towels, wipe fish fillets and set aside.
2. Core, seed, and halve red peppers. Cut lengthwise into ¼-inch-wide julienne strips. Peel and mince garlic.
3. In medium-size skillet, heat olive oil over high heat for 1 minute. Reduce heat to medium, add red peppers, and sauté, stirring with wooden spatula, until tender, about 8 minutes. Add garlic, oregano, salt and pepper to taste, and cook 30 seconds, stirring with wooden spatula. Remove pan from heat and set aside.
4. Peel red onion. With chef's knife, cut in half lengthwise, then cut crosswise into paper-thin slices.
5. Wearing thin rubber gloves, rinse chili pepper if using, and dry with paper towel. With paring knife, cut open pepper, and remove seeds with tip of blade. With chef's knife, mince chili.
6. Preheat oven to 450 degrees.
7. Cut four 12 x 16-inch pieces of baking parchment or heavy-duty aluminum foil. Place 1 fillet in center of each

piece. Season each fillet with salt and pepper to taste and top with 2 or 3 slices of onion, one quarter of sautéed red pepper strips, and one quarter of minced chili pepper, if using. Dot each fillet with ½ tablespoon butter.

8. Fold parchment or foil over fillets and seal by folding over edges.

9. Place packages on cookie sheet and bake 8 minutes.

10. Warm dinner plates under hot running water and dry.

11. Remove fish from oven. Slit packets open and slide fish and juices out onto warm plates.

Polenta with Butter and Cheese

1 cup yellow cornmeal
1 teaspoon salt
2 sticks unsalted butter (at room temperature), approximately
¼ pound Parmesan cheese
Watercress sprigs for garnish (optional)

1. Bring water to a simmer in bottom of double boiler unit. In large saucepan, bring 2½ cups of water to a boil, then reduce to a simmer.

2. In medium-size bowl, combine cornmeal, salt, and 1½ cups cold water, stirring with wooden spoon. To the simmering water, add cornmeal mixture all at once, stirring and flattening any lumps with back of spoon.

3. Immediately transfer cornmeal mixture to top of double boiler and cook over simmering water, stirring frequently, until polenta is thick enough to hold spoon upright, 45 minutes.

4. Grate enough Parmesan cheese to measure ½ cup.

5. Wash, pat dry, and trim watercress sprigs, if using.

6. Butter a large cutting board or cover 18-inch square section of counter with buttered wax paper.

7. Remove polenta from heat. Using wooden spoon, stir in butter, 2 tablespoons at a time, until thoroughly incorporated. Add cheese and stir until blended.

8. Transfer polenta to buttered board or wax paper. Shape into 12 x 14 x 1-inch rectangle. Let rest 1 minute.

9. With chef's knife, cut into 4 equal pieces. With metal spatula, transfer to dinner plates and garnish with watercress sprigs, if desired.

Marinated Salad

Small onion
½ cup dried black beans
¼ cup balsamic vinegar
Salt
Freshly ground pepper
½ cup virgin olive oil
½ pound mushrooms
½ pound broccoli
½ pint cherry tomatoes
Medium-size cucumber
4 to 8 large, light green leaves Boston lettuce

1. Peel onion, but do not slice. In small saucepan, cover black beans with 4 inches of cold water. Add onion and

bring to a boil over medium-high heat. Reduce heat and simmer 40 to 50 minutes, or until beans are *al dente*.

2. In small bowl, combine vinegar with salt and pepper to taste. In a slow, steady stream, add oil, whisking vigorously until combined.

3. Wipe mushrooms clean with damp paper towels. With paring knife, cut mushrooms into ¼-inch slices and place in large bowl. Pour in half the salad dressing and toss mushrooms to coat.

4. In medium-size saucepan over medium-high heat, bring 6 cups water to a boil.

5. Wash broccoli and cut into florets. Add to boiling water and cook just until tender, 3 to 5 minutes.

6. Rinse cherry tomatoes and pat dry with paper towels. With chef's knife, slice in half vertically.

7. Using vegetable peeler, peel cucumber. Cut cucumber in half lengthwise. Using spoon, scoop out seeds and discard. Cut cucumber into ¼-inch-thick crescents.

8. In colander, drain broccoli and refresh under cold running water. Pat dry with paper towels and trim off stems on diagonal.

9. In colander, drain black beans, shaking colander gently to drain off liquid. Discard onion.

10. To large bowl with mushrooms, add black beans, broccoli, tomatoes, and cucumber, and toss to combine. Add remaining dressing and toss.

11. Rinse lettuce and dry in salad spinner or pat dry with paper towels. Divide lettuce among 4 individual salad bowls and top each with salad.

ADDED TOUCH

These rich, buttery coconut cookies, sprinkled with confectioners' sugar, could be complemented by a creamy fruit-flavored spumoni (an Italian ice cream).

Coconut Butter Cookies

2 sticks unsalted butter
½ cup confectioners' sugar, approximately
2 cups flour
¼ teaspoon salt
1 teaspoon vanilla extract
1 cup grated moist coconut, fresh or packaged

1. Cut butter into tablespoon-size pieces.

2. In large mixing bowl, using electric mixer at high speed, combine butter and ½ cup sugar until completely blended. Reduce speed to low. Add flour, salt, and vanilla, and continue beating until well-blended. Add coconut and blend.

3. Form dough into 2 long rolls about 1½ inches in diameter and wrap in wax paper. Chill at least 2 hours.

4. Preheat oven to 350 degrees.

5. Cut rolls into ¼-inch-thick rounds and place 1 inch apart on cookie sheet. Bake until lightly browned, about 15 minutes.

6. With metal spatula, transfer hot cookies to wire rack to cool. While cookies are warm, shake confectioners' sugar through sieve held over cookies.

Fresh Tomato and Fennel Soup
Trout Baked in Coarse Salt / Chard in Butter and Garlic
New Potatoes with Basil

When you serve this informal meal, bring the soup to the table in a tureen. Arrange the salt-baked trout on a bed of coarse salt *on a large oval platter. The potatoes and the chard come in separate serving dishes.*

The ancient Chinese probably devised this technique of cooking food packed in salt. One advantage of this method is the brief cooking time: at high heat, the salt seals in the food, trapping moisture and flavor. The salt does not flavor the trout, which emerges from the salt delicately cooked in its own juices.

Swiss chard is not Swiss at all, but a native of the Mediterranean area. Related to beetroot, chard is esteemed for its earthy, spinach-like taste. Its dark green leaves cook just like spinach, too; the white stems, which are left over in this recipe, cook like celery or asparagus. Select chard that has fresh crisp leaves without any signs of wilting or discoloration. Refrigerate unwashed chard in a plastic bag, where it will last for three to five days.

Use fresh basil or any other fresh herb on the potatoes, but chop it at the last minute to prevent wilting. The potatoes themselves should be tiny and sweet, preferably part of a spring crop.

WHAT TO DRINK

The vivid flavors of this menu require a dry, fruity wine, such as an Italian Pinot Grigio or Pinot Bianco.

SHOPPING LIST AND STAPLES

4 whole trout or red snapper (each about 8 ounces), cleaned and gutted
6 medium-size tomatoes (about 3¾ pounds total weight)
3 bunches red or green chard (about 3½ pounds total weight)
12 small new red potatoes, each about 1½ inches in diameter (about 1½ pounds total weight)
Large onion
1 clove garlic
Small fennel bulb (about 8 ounces), or 1 heaped tablespoon fennel seeds
Small bunch basil
Small bunch parsley (optional)
1 lemon
1 stick plus 2 tablespoons unsalted butter
½ cup milk
1 cup chicken stock, preferably homemade (see page 13), or canned
¼ cup plus 3 tablespoons extra-virgin olive oil,
5 pounds coarse (kosher) salt
Salt and freshly ground pepper

UTENSILS

Food processor or blender
Large saucepan with cover
2 medium-size saucepans, one with cover
15 x 17-inch shallow baking pan
2 platters
Large bowl
Colander
Large sieve

Measuring cups and spoons
Chef's knife
Paring knife
2 wooden spoons
Ladle
2 metal spatulas
Wooden spatula
Garlic press (optional)
Juicer
Pastry brush

START-TO-FINISH STEPS

1. Follow soup recipe steps 1 and 2.
2. While onion is cooking, follow chard recipe steps 1 and 2, and fish recipe steps 1 and 2.
3. Follow soup recipe step 3.
4. While soup is simmering, follow chard recipe step 3 and potatoes recipe steps 1 and 2.
5. Follow fish recipe step 3 and chard recipe step 4.
6. Follow soup recipe step 4, potatoes recipe step 3, and fish recipe step 4.
7. Follow soup recipe steps 5 and 6. While heating soup, follow fish recipe step 5 and potatoes recipe step 4.
8. Follow soup recipe steps 7 and 8, and serve.
9. Follow potatoes recipe step 5 and chard recipe step 5.
10. Follow fish recipe steps 6 and 7, and chard recipe step 6.
11. Follow fish recipe step 8, potatoes recipe step 6, and serve with chard.

RECIPES

Fresh Tomato and Fennel Soup

6 medium-size tomatoes (about 3¾ pounds total weight)
Large onion
Small fennel bulb (about 8 ounces), or 1 heaped tablespoon fennel seeds
4 tablespoons unsalted butter
1 cup chicken stock
1 teaspoon salt
Freshly ground pepper
½ cup milk

1. Rinse, core, and coarsely chop tomatoes. Peel and slice onion. If using fresh fennel, rinse bulb and slice thinly, reserving sprigs for garnish, if desired.
2. In medium-size saucepan melt butter over medium heat. Add sliced onion and cook, stirring with wooden spatula, until wilted, about 8 minutes.
3. Add tomatoes, fennel or fennel seeds, stock, salt, and pepper to taste. Cover and bring to a boil over high heat. Reduce heat and simmer until fennel is tender, about 20 minutes.
4. Remove from heat and cool 5 minutes.
5. Using ladle, transfer mixture in 3-cup batches to food processor or blender, process until smooth, and transfer to large bowl. Rinse saucepan. Place sieve over saucepan

and, using back of spoon, push mixture through sieve into saucepan.

6. Add milk to soup and bring to a simmer over medium-high heat.

7. Heat tureen under hot running water and dry.

8. Check and correct seasoning. Ladle soup into tureen and serve.

Trout Baked in Coarse Salt

5 pounds coarse (kosher) salt
4 whole trout or red snapper (each about 8 ounces), cleaned and gutted
¼ cup extra-virgin olive oil
Parsley sprigs for garnish (optional)

1. Cover bottom of 15 x 17-inch shallow baking pan with 3½ pounds coarse salt.

2. Wash fish and pat dry with paper towels.

3. Preheat oven to 500 degrees.

4. Place baking pan in oven.

5. Remove pan from oven and arrange fish on hot salt, ensuring that they are not touching. Cover fish completely with remaining salt. Bake 15 minutes.

6. Heat platter under hot running water and dry.

7. Remove fish from oven and crack off top salt. Gently lift fish out with 2 metal spatulas and place on warmed platter. With pastry brush, remove discolored salt from top of fish and from belly cavity.

8. Discard discolored salt in baking pan and transfer remaining salt to another platter. With 2 spatulas, transfer fish onto bed of salt. Drizzle olive oil over fish and garnish with parsley sprigs, if desired.

Chard in Butter and Garlic

3 bunches red or green chard (about 3½ pounds total weight)
6 tablespoons unsalted butter
1 clove garlic
Salt
Freshly ground pepper
1 lemon

1. In large covered saucepan, bring 2 quarts water and 2 teaspoons salt to a boil over high heat.

2. Trim green chard leaves from central stems, reserving stems for another use. Rinse leaves and shake off excess water.

3. Drop leaves into boiling water and cook just until tender, 5 to 7 minutes.

4. In colander, drain chard, refresh under cold running water and, with wooden spoon, press out extra liquid.

5. In same saucepan, melt butter over medium heat. Peel garlic and put through garlic press or mince finely. Sauté in butter about 1 minute.

6. Add chard and salt and pepper to taste, and squeeze in lemon juice to taste. With wooden spoon or spatula, toss gently to mix and sauté until heated through, 2 to 3 minutes. Transfer to serving plate.

New Potatoes with Basil

12 small new red potatoes, each about 1½ inches in diameter (about 1½ pounds total weight)
8 fresh basil leaves
3 tablespoons extra-virgin olive oil
Salt
Freshly ground pepper

1. Wash potatoes and drain in colander.

2. Wash basil leaves and pat dry with paper towels. Using paring knife, cut basil into fine strips, 1/16 to 1/8 inch thick.

3. In medium-size saucepan bring 1½ quarts water to a boil over high heat.

4. Add potatoes to boiling water. Reduce heat to medium and simmer, covered, until fork pierces potatoes easily, 10 to 15 minutes.

5. In colander, drain potatoes. Halve potatoes, return to saucepan, and cover.

6. Uncover pan, add oil, basil, and salt and pepper to taste, and toss with 2 wooden spoons. Transfer to serving bowl.

ADDED TOUCH

This light, fudgy cake will have a cracked top. Be careful not to overbake it; the cake should be moist.

Carlo's Chocolate Earthquake Cake

¾ pound semi-sweet chocolate
1 stick unsalted butter
4 eggs, at room temperature
2 cups confectioners' sugar
¼ cup potato flour or all-purpose flour
2 tablespoons grated orange rind
1 teaspoon vanilla extract

1. Preheat oven to 250 degrees.

2. In top of double boiler, combine chocolate and butter. Place over almost simmering water and stir until just melted, 4 to 5 minutes. With rubber spatula, scrape into medium-size bowl and let cool slightly.

3. Generously butter and flour 8-inch round cake pan. Cut round of baking parchment or wax paper and cover bottom of pan.

4. Wash upper half of double boiler and crack eggs into it. Place over simmering water and, with electric mixer at high speed, beat until approximately double in volume and eggs are light-colored, creamy, and form soft peaks, 10 to 15 minutes.

5. Sift sugar and then sift sugar together with flour.

6. Pour chocolate mixture into egg mixture and, with wooden spoon, stir gently to combine. Add sugar and flour mixture, one third at a time, stirring well with metal spoon after each addition. Stir in orange rind and vanilla extract.

7. Pour batter into prepared cake pan, place in oven, and bake 30 minutes. Let cool before removing from pan. Cake will have texture of a light, very fudgy brownie.

Josephine Araldo

MENU 1 (Right)
Quenelles with Shallot Sauce
Potatoes with Onions and Cheese
Sautéed Carrots and Grapes

MENU 2
Avocado and Potato Soup
Fillets of Sole in Wine Sauce
Zucchini Merveille

MENU 3
Lima Bean Soup
Whiting with Lemon Sauce
Cucumbers and Brussels Sprouts

A star pupil of Cordon Bleu chef Henri-Paul Pellaprat, Josephine Araldo nonetheless attributes her imaginative combinations of fruits and vegetables to her grandmother, who not only taught young Josephine to cook but to respect fresh food. In fact, all the vegetable recipes in these three menus were inspired by her grandmother. The most unusual combination, and a favorite of Josephine Araldo's, is the carrots with grapes that accompany the quenelles and potatoes in Menu 1.

From her grandmother she also learned kitchen economy, and she believes that a sign of a truly good cook is the ability to work creatively with leftovers. The fish and the vegetable recipes of Menu 2 typify her waste-not philosophy. The cooking liquid for the sole fillets is the base for its flavorful sauce, and the sliced zucchini are cooked in and served with the same herb- and wine-enriched stock.

A master of haute cuisine (she was crowned with her white chef's toque by M. Pellaprat himself), she nonetheless describes herself as a practical cook who uses simple tools and basic techniques, fish being a favorite food because it requires so little treatment. She also sings while she cooks. "Singing makes you cook better," she says. She shops early every day to select quality foods at the best price. She avoids using costly ingredients when less expensive ones will do. For instance, in Menu 3 she features whiting, an ordinary fish often considered inelegant. Here, served with a delicate lemon sauce and accompanied by lima bean soup and a side dish of cucumbers and Brussels sprouts flavored with gin or juniper berries, the whiting becomes a company meal.

Formal dinnerware underlines the elegance of quenelles served with a creamy herb sauce. Browned sliced potatoes with onions and cheese and sliced carrots with grapes are perfect partners.

Quenelles with Shallot Sauce
Potatoes with Onions and Cheese
Sautéed Carrots and Grapes

You cannot make *quenelles*—classic French fish dumplings—without a food processor, which shortens the otherwise lengthy preparation time to minutes. A blender is not a substitute because its blades will clog with the fish flesh. The fish paste must be packed in ice to be firm enough to absorb the cream before poaching. Quenelles are cooked when they float to the surface.

WHAT TO DRINK

A Graves or an Entre-Duex-Mers, both medium-bodied, flavorful wines, would be good with the quenelles.

SHOPPING LIST AND STAPLES

¾ pound sea or bay scallops
¾ pound fillets of sole
2 pounds carrots
4 medium-size potatoes (about 1½ pounds total weight)
2 medium-size onions
1 clove garlic
3 to 4 shallots
Small bunch parsley
Small bunch dill
Small bunch mint
½ pound seedless grapes, preferably red
1 lemon
1 egg
1 pint heavy cream
1 stick plus 2 tablespoons unsalted butter
¼ pound Swiss cheese, preferably imported, thinly sliced
1¾ cup chicken stock, preferably homemade
   (see page 13), or canned
½ cup fish stock or 8-ounce bottle clam juice
2 tablespoons flour
1 tablespoon sugar
1 bay leaf
Salt and freshly ground white pepper
1 cup dry Sauterne
1 tablespoon Cognac

UTENSILS

Food processor
Large skillet
Medium-size skillet
Medium-size saucepan with cover
2 small saucepans
1½-quart ovenproof baking dish
Jelly-roll pan
Platter
2 large mixing bowls plus additional slightly larger bowl
2 small bowls
Colander
Measuring cups and spoons
Chef's knife
Paring knife
Slotted spoon
3 wooden spoons
Rubber spatula
Whisk
2 tablespoons
1 glass
Vegetable peeler

START-TO-FINISH STEPS

1. Follow quenelles recipe steps 1 through 3.
2. Follow potatoes recipe steps 1 through 7.
3. Prepare herbs for quenelles and sauce. Follow quenelles recipe steps 4 through 8.
4. Follow sauce recipe steps 1 and 2.
5. Follow carrots recipe steps 1 and 2.
6. Follow quenelles recipe steps 9 through 13. While first batch of quenelles is poaching, follow carrots recipe step 3. While second batch is poaching, follow carrots recipe step 4 and potatoes recipe step 8. While third batch is poaching, follow sauce recipe step 3, and while fourth batch is poaching, follow sauce recipe step 4.
7. Follow potatoes recipe step 9, and lower heat to 200 degrees, leaving oven door ajar for 1 minute.
8. Place quenelles in oven, step 14.
9. Follow carrots recipe step 5, sauce recipe step 5, quenelles recipe step 15, and serve with potatoes.

RECIPES

Quenelles with Shallot Sauce

¾ pound sea or bay scallops
¾ pound fillets of sole
1½ to 2 cups heavy cream
Salt
½ tablespoon finely minced shallot
1 clove garlic, peeled and finely minced
¼ teaspoon freshly ground white pepper

1 egg
1 tablespoon Cognac
2 tablespoons chopped parsley
Shallot sauce (see following recipe)

1. In colander, rinse scallops. Pat dry with paper towels.
2. Wipe fillets with damp paper towels. With chef's knife, cut each fillet crosswise into thirds.
3. Combine scallops and sole in bowl of food processor, cover, and place in freezer to chill at least 15 minutes. Place cream and large mixing bowl in refrigerator to chill.
4. Remove food processor bowl from freezer, add ½ teaspoon salt, and process fish until thick and smooth.
5. Set chilled mixing bowl in another slightly larger bowl filled with ice. Scrape fish mixture into bowl. Add shallot, garlic, salt, and pepper, and beat until blended.
6. In small bowl, beat egg with fork. Add egg to fish mixture and beat until blended.
7. Add cream to fish mixture ¼ cup at a time, beating after each addition until totally incorporated. Stop adding cream when fish mixture no longer absorbs it.
8. Add Cognac and parsley, and beat until blended. Cover bowl and chill until ready to proceed.
9. In large skillet, bring 2 inches of water and 1 teaspoon salt to a boil.
10. While water is coming to a boil, line jelly-roll pan with aluminum foil and line platter with paper towels. Fill a glass with cold water and in it place 2 tablespoons, bowls down. Remove fish mixture from refrigerator. Adjust heat under skillet so that water barely shivers.
11. Remove tablespoons from glass. With one spoon, pick up a rounded spoonful of fish mixture and smooth the top with the back of the other. Then, with the second spoon, nudge the quenelle off the first spoon into the skillet. Working quickly, repeat, always rewetting the spoons, until about one quarter of the mixture has been used. You should have 10 to 12 quenelles. (As you add quenelles, adjust heat to keep water at the barest simmer, being careful not to let it boil.) Poach quenelles 2 to 3 minutes.
12. With slotted spoon, transfer quenelles to paper-towel-lined platter and then to jelly-roll pan. Cover jelly-roll pan loosely with foil and keep warm on stove top.
13. Repeat procedure three more times.
14. When all quenelles have been cooked, place jelly-roll pan in 200-degree oven until ready to serve.
15. When ready to serve, remove quenelles from oven, divide among 4 dinner plates, and top with sauce.

Shallot Sauce

3 tablespoons unsalted butter
2 tablespoons finely minced shallots
1 cup dry Sauterne
½ cup fish stock or clam juice
¼ teaspoon freshly ground white pepper
2 tablespoons flour
2 tablespoons chopped dill
2 tablespoons chopped parsley
1 to 2 tablespoons heavy cream

1. In small saucepan, melt 1 tablespoon butter over medium heat. Add shallots and sauté 2 minutes.
2. Slowly stir in Sauterne. Raise heat to medium-high and reduce liquid by half, about 5 minutes. Add fish stock and pepper, and stir to combine. Reduce heat to medium.
3. In small bowl, cream remaining 2 tablespoons butter with back of spoon until soft. Add flour and blend until totally incorporated to form *beurre manié*.
4. Add *beurre manié* to sauce 1 teaspoon at a time, whisking after each addition until blended before adding more. Simmer 2 minutes and keep warm over very low heat.
5. Just before serving, stir in dill, parsley, and cream.

Potatoes with Onions and Cheese

4 medium-size potatoes (about 1½ pounds total weight)
1 cup chicken stock, approximately
2 medium-size onions
2 to 3 tablespoons unsalted butter
¼ pound Swiss cheese, preferably imported, thinly sliced
Salt and freshly ground white pepper

1. Preheat oven to 375 degrees.
2. Fill large bowl with cold water. Peel potatoes and drop them in bowl as you peel them.
3. With chef's knife, cut potatoes into ⅛-inch slices.
4. In small saucepan, heat stock over medium heat.
5. Peel and chop onions. In medium-size skillet, melt butter over medium heat. Add onions and sauté 2 minutes.
6. Meanwhile, butter 1½-quart ovenproof baking dish.
7. In baking dish, layer potatoes, cheese, and onions, adding salt and pepper to taste after you form each layer. Pour in enough hot stock to fill dish three quarters full. Cover dish with aluminum foil and bake 30 minutes.
8. Uncover potatoes, and bake 10 minutes longer, or until brown crust has formed.
9. Remove potatoes from oven, cover loosely with foil, and keep warm on stove top.

Sautéed Carrots and Grapes

1½ cups seedless grapes, preferably red (about ½ pound)
2 pounds carrots
4 tablespoons unsalted butter
¾ cup chicken stock
Salt and freshly ground white pepper
1 tablespoon sugar
1 tablespoon chopped fresh mint
1 teaspoon chopped fresh parsley

1. Remove stems from grapes. In colander, rinse grapes and drain. Pat dry with paper towels and set aside.
2. Peel carrots and cut into ½-inch rounds.
3. In medium-size saucepan, melt 3 tablespoons butter over medium-high heat. Add carrots and sauté 1 minute.
4. Stir in stock and salt and pepper to taste. Raise heat to high and bring to a boil. Reduce heat to low and cook carrots, covered, 10 minutes or just until tender.
5. Remove pan from heat. Add grapes and sugar, and stir gently to combine. Stir in remaining tablespoon butter, mint, and parsley. Divide among 4 dinner plates.

Avocado and Potato Soup
Fillets of Sole in Wine Sauce
Zucchini Merveille

Mugs of creamy avocado soup, garnished with slices of ripe avocado and chopped chives, introduce this simple meal: fillets of sole in wine sauce and a colorful medley of gently cooked fresh vegetables.

For this meal, sole fillets bake in a glass dish with chopped onion, carrot, and herbs, all of which enhance the mild flavor of the fish. Cover the fillets with a layer of buttered wax paper, then with a layer of foil to prevent the sole from discoloring.

Although there are numerous varieties of avocados, most taste very much alike. For the soup, select avocados that yield to slight pressure and are free of blemishes. To ripen an avocado, place it in a paper bag and leave it at room temperature. Test for ripeness by inserting a toothpick or slender skewer into the avocado at its stem end. The avocado is ripe if the toothpick moves easily. Once ripened, avocados should be refrigerated.

WHAT TO DRINK

For a change of pace, try a young Spanish white wine from the Rioja district. A California Pinot Blanc would also go well with this meal.

SHOPPING LIST AND STAPLES

Four ½-inch-thick fillets of sole (each about 7 ounces)
2 large avocados plus 1 small avocado (optional)
2 large tomatoes, or 16-ounce can Italian plum tomatoes
1½ pounds zucchini
Medium-size carrot
4 medium-size potatoes (about 1½ pounds total weight)
12 white boiling onions plus 1 medium-size onion
   or 3 large onions plus 1 medium-size
1 clove garlic
Small bulb fennel with leaves
Small bunch fresh thyme, or 1 teaspoon plus 1 pinch of
   dried
Small bunch fresh dill
Small bunch fresh marjoram, or 1 pinch of dried
Small bunch fresh oregano, or 1 pinch of dried
Small bunch fresh chives or 2-ounce container frozen
1 lemon
4 cups chicken stock, preferably homemade (see page 13),
   or canned
2 tablespoons unsalted butter, approximately
2 tablespoons olive oil
2 tablespoons flour
1 bay leaf
Salt
Freshly ground pepper

½ cup dry sherry
1½ cups white wine

UTENSILS

Food processor or blender
Large saucepan with cover
2 medium-size saucepans, one with cover
Small saucepan
13 x 9 x 2-inch heatproof glass baking dish
Medium-size bowl
Small bowl
Colander
Measuring cups and spoons
Chef's knife
Paring knife
Slotted spoon
2 wooden spoons
Metal spatula
Rubber spatula
Grater
Juicer (optional)
Whisk
Fine-mesh sieve
Vegetable peeler

START-TO-FINISH STEPS

1. Follow soup recipe steps 1 through 3.
2. While potatoes are cooking, follow zucchini recipe steps 1 through 4.
3. Chop chives for soup recipe and prepare vegetables and herbs for sole recipe.
4. Follow sole recipe step 1.
5. Follow soup recipe steps 4 through 7.
6. Follow zucchini recipe step 5 and sole recipe steps 2 and 3.
7. While sole is baking, follow zucchini recipe step 6.
8. Follow sole recipe steps 4 and 5 and soup recipe steps 8 and 9.
9. Follow sole recipe steps 6 and 7, soup recipe step 10, and serve with zucchini.

RECIPES

Avocado and Potato Soup

4 medium-size potatoes (about 1½ pounds total weight)
2 large avocados plus 1 small avocado for garnish
    (optional)
¼ cup finely chopped chives plus 2 teaspoons chopped
    chives for garnish (optional)
3 cups chicken stock
½ cup dry sherry
Salt
Freshly ground pepper

1. In medium-size saucepan, bring 2 quarts of water to a boil over high heat.
2. Fill medium-size bowl with cold water. Peel and quarter potatoes, and drop them in bowl as you peel them.
3. Add potatoes to boiling water, cover, and cook until tender, 15 to 20 minutes, or until potatoes can be pierced easily with tip of knife.
4. In colander, drain potatoes and return to warm pan.
5. Peel 2 large avocados and halve lengthwise, cutting around pit. Twist to separate halves. Remove pit and discard. Cut flesh into chunks and place in bowl of food processor or blender.
6. If using food processor, add potatoes and chives, and process until mashed. If using blender, add potatoes, chives, and 1 cup of stock, and process until smooth.
7. With rubber spatula, scrape mixture into pan in which potatoes were cooked. Add stock, sherry, and salt and pepper to taste, and stir until blended.
8. Stirring frequently with wooden spoon, bring soup just to a simmer over medium-high heat.
9. While soup is heating, peel, halve, and pit small avocado, if using for garnish. Cut each half lengthwise into four ½-inch-thick slices.
10. Divide soup among individual bowls or mugs and, if desired, garnish with avocado slices and remaining chopped chives.

Fillets of Sole in Wine Sauce

Four ½-inch-thick fillets of sole (each about 7 ounces)
2 tablespoons unsalted butter, approximately
1 cup chopped onion
½ cup chopped carrot
1 tablespoon chopped fresh thyme, or 1 teaspoon dried
1 tablespoon chopped fennel leaves
1 tablespoon snipped fresh dill
1 bay leaf
½ cup white wine
Salt
Freshly ground pepper
2 tablespoons flour

1. Preheat oven to 375 degrees. Wipe fillets with damp paper towels.
2. Cut a sheet of wax paper to fit baking dish and butter lightly.
3. In heatproof glass baking dish, place onion, carrot, thyme, fennel, dill, and bay leaf. Top vegetables and herbs with fillets. Add wine, ½ cup water, and salt and freshly ground pepper to taste. Cover with wax paper, buttered side down. Top with a sheet of aluminum foil and crimp foil around edges of the dish. Bake 12 to 15 minutes or until fish barely flakes when tested with tip of sharp knife.
4. In small bowl, cream 2 tablespoons butter with back of spoon until soft. Add flour and, with fingers or back of spoon, blend until totally incorporated to form *beurre manié*.
5. Place dinner plates under hot running water to warm.
6. Just before fish is done, dry plates. Remove fish from oven and, with metal spatula, transfer fillets to warm dinner plates. Drain cooking liquid through a fine-mesh sieve set over small saucepan. Add *beurre manié* to pan

and whisk until blended, 2 to 3 minutes. Taste for seasoning.

7. Spoon sauce over each fillet.

Zucchini Merveille

1½ pounds zucchini
12 white boiling onions or 3 large onions
1 clove garlic
2 large tomatoes or 16-ounce can Italian plum tomatoes
1 sprig fresh thyme, or 1 pinch of dried
1 sprig fresh oregano, or 1 pinch of dried
1 sprig fresh marjoram, or 1 pinch of dried
1 lemon
2 tablespoons olive oil
1 cup chicken stock
1 cup white wine
Salt
Freshly ground pepper

1. Fill medium-size saucepan with water to within 2 inches of the rim and bring to a boil over high heat.

2. While water is coming to a boil, wash zucchini, pat dry with paper towels, and cut on diagonal into ½-inch-thick slices. Peel onions and, if using large onions, quarter them. Peel and mince garlic.

3. Drop tomatoes into boiling water and let stand 1 minute. With slotted spoon, transfer to colander, and cool under cold running water. Peel, halve, and seed. Cut into quarters. If using canned tomatoes, drain.

4. If using fresh herbs, strip leaves from stems. Grate lemon zest, then slice lemon in half and juice.

5. In large saucepan, heat 2 tablespoons olive oil briefly over medium-high heat. Add onions and garlic, and sauté, stirring frequently with wooden spoon, 4 to 5 minutes.

6. Add tomatoes, stock, wine, lemon juice, lemon zest, herbs, and salt and pepper to taste and stir to combine. Bring to a boil and add zucchini. Reduce heat to medium-low and cook just until zucchini are tender, about 10 minutes. Cover pan partially, remove from heat, and keep warm until ready to serve.

ADDED TOUCH

This version of chocolate soufflé bakes while you eat dinner or while your guests have after-dinner coffee.

Chocolate Soufflé

2 tablespoons brewed coffee or 1 teaspoon instant freeze-
    dried granules
4 large eggs, at room temperature
3 tablespoons unsalted butter, approximately
½ cup sugar
Two 1-ounce squares unsweetened chocolate
¼ cup all-purpose flour
1 cup milk
1 teaspoon vanilla extract
¼ teaspoon salt
¼ teaspoon cream of tartar
½ pint heavy cream (optional)

1. Reserve 2 tablespoons coffee from your morning cup or, in small saucepan, bring 2 tablespoons water to a boil and add 1 teaspoon instant freeze-dried granules. Set aside.

2. Separate eggs, placing 3 whites in large non-aluminum bowl and 4 yolks in small bowl, and reserving extra white for another use.

3. Lightly butter 1-quart soufflé dish. Sprinkle butter with 2 tablespoons sugar. Tilt dish on its side and roll it around to distribute sugar evenly.

4. In lower half of double boiler, bring 1 inch of water to a simmer over medium heat. In upper half of double boiler, combine chocolate and coffee, and set over lower half, stirring occasionally with whisk, until chocolate is melted, 3 to 5 minutes.

5. When chocolate has melted, add butter, 1 tablespoon at a time, whisking after each addition until butter is incorporated before adding more.

6. Add flour and stir until blended. Continue to cook, stirring, 4 to 5 minutes.

7. While flour-chocolate mixture is cooking, scald milk in small saucepan over medium heat bringing it just up to— but not to—the boiling point. Preheat oven to 400 degrees.

8. Remove chocolate mixture from heat, but leave lower half of double boiler on burner. Add ¼ cup plus 1 tablespoon sugar and scalded milk and stir until blended.

9. Return upper half of double boiler to lower half and cook, stirring constantly, until very thick, 7 to 10 minutes. Again remove from heat and beat mixture about 1 minute.

10. Beat in egg yolks, one at a time, until totally incorporated. Beat in vanilla extract.

11. To large bowl with egg whites, add salt. With whisk or electric beater at medium speed, beat whites until foamy. Add cream of tartar and beat whites until soft peaks form. Add remaining tablespoon sugar and continue to beat just until whites stand in stiff, shiny peaks. Do not overbeat.

12. With rubber spatula, scoop up one-third of beaten whites and fold into cooled chocolate. Then with spatula carefully fold in remaining whites.

13. Gently turn mixture into prepared soufflé dish, filling dish three quarters full. With knife, make a ½-inch-deep cut around circumference of batter, 1 inch in from edge of dish. The crust will break at this point and form a taller center, creating a top-hat effect when the soufflé has risen.

14. Place soufflé on middle shelf of preheated oven for 3 to 5 minutes, then reduce temperature to 375 degrees and bake an additional 20 minutes.

15. If using whipped cream as an accompaniment, chill mixing bowl and beaters in freezer 15 minutes before soufflé is done. Five minutes before soufflé is done, remove bowl and beaters from refrigerator and pour cream into bowl. Whip at medium speed until cream has thickened but is still soft and a little runny. Turn into serving bowl.

16. Remove soufflé from oven and bring to the table immediately. Using 2 large spoons, serve each diner a portion of the crust and a portion of the interior of the soufflé. If using whipped cream, spoon a few tablespoons alongside each serving.

Lima Bean Soup
Whiting with Lemon Sauce
Cucumbers and Brussels Sprouts

Whiting, which may flake apart during cooking, requires gentle handling when fried, as in this recipe. The puréed lima bean soup is flavored with fresh herbs and thickened with *crème fraîche*, a cultured cream with a slightly tart, nutty taste. Once a French specialty but now produced in the United States, crème fraîche is hard to find ready-made except at gourmet shops and certain supermarkets, but you can make a reasonable facsimile of it yourself (see page 56).

WHAT TO DRINK

An Italian Soave would be ideal here, or try a dry California Chenin-Blanc—both are soft and medium bodied.

SHOPPING LIST AND STAPLES

4 fillets of whiting (silver hake) (about 1½ pounds total weight)
1½ pounds fresh Brussels sprouts or two 10-ounce packages frozen
2½ cups fresh lima beans
Medium-size onion plus small onion
Small carrot
2 cucumbers (about 1½ pounds total weight)
1 red radish (optional)
1 fennel bulb with leaves, or small bunch fresh dill or 1 tablespoon dill seeds
Small bunch fresh tarragon, or 1 teaspoon dried
Small bunch fresh parsley or chervil
1 lemon
1 lime
3 eggs
½ pint heavy cream (if making crème fraîche)
½ pint sour cream (if making crème fraîche)
½ pint commercial crème fraîche if not using homemade
2 sticks plus 5 tablespoons unsalted butter, approximately
3 cups chicken stock, preferably homemade (page 13), or canned
1 tablespoon vegetable oil
1 baguette
½ cup flour
1 teaspoon sugar
6 or 7 juniper berries, or 2 to 3 tablespoons gin
½ teaspoon celery seeds
Pinch of cloves
Salt and freshly ground pepper

Offer this casual meal buffet style: Set out a tureen of lima bean soup with a bowl of sautéed cucumbers and Brussels sprouts. Arrange the whiting fillets on a platter, and serve the sauce separately.

Food processor or blender
2 heavy-gauge skillets, one with cover
2 medium-size saucepans
Two 9-inch pie pans or flat plates
Platter
2 medium-size bowls
2 small bowls
Shallow bowl
Jar with lid or small bowl (if making crème fraîche)
Colander
Measuring cups and spoons
Chef's knife
Paring knife
3 wooden spoons
Metal spatula
Melon baller (optional)

START-TO-FINISH STEPS

At least 8 hours ahead: If making crème fraîche, combine ½ cup sour cream with 1 cup heavy cream in jar with lid or in small bowl. Blend thoroughly, cover partially, and set in warm (but not hot) place for about 8 hours or until mixture thickens. Cover and refrigerate. Crème fraîche will keep about 10 days.

1. Follow lima bean soup recipe steps 1 through 3.
2. While lima beans are cooking, prepare herbs for cucumbers and Brussels sprouts and follow recipe step 1.
3. If using fresh Brussels sprouts, follow cucumbers and Brussels sprouts recipe step 2.
4. Follow soup recipe step 4.
5. Cut baguette in half, reserving one half for another use. Process enough bread in blender to yield 1 cup crumbs.
6. Follow whiting recipe steps 1 through 5.
7. Follow cucumbers recipe steps 3 through 8; if using frozen sprouts, omit steps 5 and 7. Turn off heat.
8. Follow soup recipe steps 5 through 8 and serve.
9. Follow cucumbers recipe step 9.
10. While sprouts are cooking, remove whiting from refrigerator and follow whiting recipe steps 6 through 8.
11. Follow cucumbers recipe step 10, whiting recipe step 9, and serve.

RECIPES

Lima Bean Soup

Small onion
Small carrot
1 tablespoon unsalted butter
3 cups chicken stock
2½ cups fresh lima beans
1 tablespoon chopped fresh tarragon, or 1 teaspoon dried
1 tablespoon chopped fresh parsley or chervil
Salt and freshly ground pepper
1 egg
⅓ cup crème fraîche

1. Peel and chop onion and carrot.
2. In medium-size saucepan, melt butter over medium heat. Add onion and carrot, and sauté, stirring with wooden spoon, until onion is translucent, 4 to 5 minutes.
3. Add 1 cup stock to pan and stir to combine. Raise heat to medium-high and bring to a boil. Add lima beans, return liquid to a boil, and cook beans 5 minutes, or until just tender.
4. Transfer beans and cooking liquid to bowl of food processor or blender. Add tarragon and parsley or chervil, and process until smooth. Return mixture to saucepan. Add remaining 2 cups stock and salt and pepper to taste, and stir until blended. Rinse processor or blender bowl and dry.
5. Bring soup to a boil, over medium-high heat, stirring frequently. Reduce heat and simmer 5 minutes.
6. While soup simmers, separate egg using 2 small bowls. With fork, beat yolk lightly; reserve white for another use. Add crème fraîche to yolk and stir with fork until blended.
7. Stirring with wooden spoon, pour yolk and crème fraîche mixture into soup and continue to stir until blended.
8. Transfer soup to tureen and serve.

Whiting with Lemon Sauce

2 sticks unsalted butter, approximately
4 fillets of whiting (silver hake) (about 1½ pounds total weight)
½ cup flour
1 cup bread crumbs
2 eggs
1 tablespoon vegetable oil
1 lemon
½ teaspoon celery seeds
Pinch of cloves
Salt and freshly ground pepper
Fennel tops for garnish (optional)
Red radish floret for garnish (optional)

1. Place 1 stick butter in medium-size bowl and set aside to soften.
2. Wipe fillets with damp paper towels.
3. Place flour and bread crumbs in separate pie pans or on flat plates. Break eggs into shallow bowl and beat with fork. Arrange dishes so that egg is in the middle.
4. One at a time, dip fillets in flour, coating both sides. Gently shake off excess and dip fillet in egg. Let excess drain off and dip fillet in bread crumbs, coating both sides. Lay breaded fillet on plate. Repeat until all fillets are breaded. Cover with plastic wrap and chill until ready to proceed.
5. Line platter with paper towels.
6. In large heavy-gauge skillet, melt oil and 2 tablespoons of butter over medium-high heat. Tilt pan back and forth to combine fats. When butter and oil begin to foam, add fillets and lower heat to medium. Cook fillets about 3 minutes per side or until light brown. Add additional butter as necessary, using up to 6 more tablespoons.

7. While fillets are browning, prepare sauce: Juice lemon. Add lemon juice, celery seeds, cloves, and salt and pepper to taste to softened butter, and beat until blended. Transfer sauce to small pitcher or sauceboat.

8. With metal spatula, transfer fillets to paper-towel-lined platter to drain.

9. Arrange fillets on serving platter and garnish with fennel tops and radish floret, if desired. Serve sauce separately.

Cucumbers and Brussels Sprouts

1½ pounds fresh Brussels sprouts, or two 10-ounce
   packages frozen
Salt
Medium-size onion
2 cucumbers (about 1½ pounds total weight)
1 lime
6 or 7 juniper berries, crushed, or 2 to 3 tablespoons gin
4 tablespoons unsalted butter
1 tablespoon chopped fresh fennel leaves, fresh snipped
   dill, or dill seeds
1 teaspoon sugar
Freshly ground pepper

1. Pick over Brussels sprouts, removing yellow leaves. In colander, rinse sprouts under cold running water and drain. Set aside.

2. If using fresh Brussels sprouts, fill medium-size saucepan with 2 quarts water, add 2 teaspoons salt, and bring to a boil over high heat.

3. Peel onion and chop coarsely.

4. Peel cucumbers and halve lengthwise. Seed cucumbers by drawing a teaspoon or melon baller down middle of cut side of each cucumber (see illustration below). Discard seeds and chop cucumber coarsely.

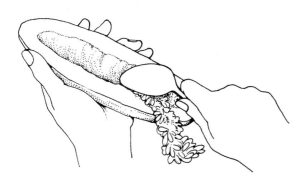

5. Add fresh sprouts to boiling water, return water to a boil, reduce to a simmer, and blanch sprouts 5 minutes.

6. While sprouts are blanching, juice lime and crush juniper berries with back of spoon.

7. In colander, drain sprouts and refresh under cold running water. Set aside.

8. In large skillet, melt butter over medium heat. Add onion and sauté, stirring with wooden spoon, until onion is translucent, 4 to 5 minutes.

9. Add cucumbers and blanched or frozen Brussels sprouts, and stir to combine. Add chopped fennel leaves or dill, juniper berries or gin, lime juice, sugar, and salt and pepper to taste. Cover skillet, reduce heat to low, and cook 7 to 10 minutes if using fresh sprouts, 3 to 5 minutes if using frozen sprouts, or until vegetables are tender but still *al dente*.

10. Turn vegetables into serving bowl.

ADDED TOUCH

For this variation on the French *petits pots de crème*, you will need small ovenproof dishes.

Breton Coffee Cream

1¼ cups light cream
1½ teaspoons instant coffee
3 eggs
⅓ cup sugar
Pinch of salt
1 teaspoon vanilla extract
½ cup heavy cream for garnish (optional)

1. Preheat oven to 350 degrees.

2. In large saucepan, over low heat, heat 1¼ cups light cream. When cream has warmed enough to be too hot for your finger, add instant coffee and, with metal spoon, stir to blend.

3. Separate eggs. Place yolks in medium-size bowl and reserve whites for another use.

4. With electric beater on high, beat yolks until thick and lemon-colored, approximately 5 minutes. Gradually add sugar and beat until well-blended and smooth. Add salt and beat to combine.

5. Lower beater speed to medium and slowly pour in cream, beating constantly, until thoroughly combined. Beat in vanilla extract.

6. Put coffee cream through fine-mesh sieve into another medium-size bowl, stirring with a spoon to help the mixture through the mesh.

7. Spoon the mixture into pots de crème dishes, small ramekins, or custard cups, cover with aluminum foil, and place ramekins in baking dish.

8. Pull oven shelf part way out and set baking dish on it. Carefully pour water around the cups to come halfway up sides of cups.

9. Close oven and bake coffee creams for 20 minutes. Remove from oven, let cool at room temperature for 30 minutes, and then refrigerate, covered, until chilled, approximately 1 hour.

10. If serving with optional whipped cream, chill bowl and beaters while coffee creams cool.

11. Five minutes before ready to serve, place heavy cream in chilled bowl and beat at medium speed until thickened but still runny, 4 to 5 minutes (a ribbon of cream will leave a trail on surface rather than immediately reincorporating into rest of cream).

12. Serve coffee creams garnished with whipped cream, if desired.

Bruce Cliborne

MENU 1 (Left)
Sautéed Scallops with White Wine Sauce
Spicy Spinach Sauté
Wild Mushroom Salad with Basil and Mint

MENU 2
Mussels and Shrimp in Coconut Cream with Mint
Stuffed Kohlrabi

MENU 3
Clams in Sesame-Ginger Sauce
Fettuccine with Garlic and Oil
Mixed Vegetables, Oriental Style

Bruce Cliborne spent his childhood summers on his grandparents' farm in rural Virginia, where they grew their own produce and raised their own beef, pork, and chicken. His grandmother's homemade sausages and freshly churned butter are some of the memories that inspire his own use of fresh, pure ingredients in cooking.

According to this cook, the culinary arts are analagous to the fine arts. As art students study the masters, beginning cooks should study the classic techniques of the world's finest chefs. With this solid grounding, cooks can be inventive. "Making good food should be challenging, intriguing, amusing, and hard work," says Bruce Cliborne.

He draws upon the cuisines of France (his major gastronomic influence), Japan, Italy, and China for inspiration, and his meals often contain elements of several, as in the menus here. In Menu 1, fresh basil, a favorite French and Italian herb, seasons the wild mushroom salad. To the French-inspired sautéed scallops, Bruce Cliborne adds hot dried chilies, which are common to Asian cooking. The two Oriental stir-fry dishes of Menu 3 are accompanied by an Italian specialty, fettuccine, with garlic as the unifying flavor for all three recipes.

The mussels and shrimp of Menu 2, an amalgam of European and Asian recipes, combines such diverse ingredients as coconut cream, mint, vermouth, olive oil, and snow peas.

For a festive meal, present scallops on a bed of sautéed spinach garnished with orange zest, and sautéed wild mushrooms on a bed of greens.

Sautéed Scallops with White Wine Sauce
Spicy Spinach Sauté
Wild Mushroom Salad with Basil and Mint

The salad for this company meal requires several unusual ingredients: arugula, lamb's tongue lettuce, and a choice of one of several varieties of fresh wild mushrooms. Arugula is a pungent Italian green that combines well with milder salad greens. Mild lamb's tongue lettuce, also known as *mâche*, grows in clumps of 10 to 15 tongue-shaped leaves. Rinse the greens well in cold water to remove any grit, wrap the clean leaves in paper towels, and refrigerate. Use them within a day or two. You can substitute Bibb or butter lettuce if you wish. If you cannot locate chanterelles, shiitake, or enokitake, substitute fresh cultivated mushrooms. Note: Unless you are an expert, under no circumstances should you use wild mushrooms picked on your own.

WHAT TO DRINK

A good-quality California Sauvignon Blanc or a good Graves would go well with the rich flavors here.

SHOPPING LIST AND STAPLES

1½ pounds plump sea scallops
⅔ pound fresh wild mushrooms, preferably chanterelles, shiitake, enokitake, or fresh cultivated mushrooms
1 pound spinach
Large bunch arugula
Large bunch lamb's tongue, or 1 head Boston or other young lettuce
Small bunch basil
Small bunch mint
4 shallots
3 cloves garlic
3 lemons
1 orange
3 eggs
2 sticks plus 2 tablespoons unsalted butter
1½ cups plus ⅓ cup olive oil
2 tablespoons white wine vinegar
1 tablespoon sherry vinegar
½ cup flour
6 whole dried chili peppers
¼ teaspoon Cayenne pepper, or ½ teaspoon red pepper flakes
Salt and freshly ground pepper
¼ cup dry white wine
1 tablespoon dry sherry

UTENSILS

2 large sauté pans
Medium-size non-aluminum saucepan with cover
Small non-aluminum saucepan
Heatproof platter
Large flat plate
2 large bowls, one heatproof
Medium-size bowl
2 small bowls
Sieve
Colander
Salad spinner (optional)
Measuring cups and spoons
Chef's knife
Paring knife
2 wooden spoons
Slotted spoon
Wooden spatula
Whisk
Juicer (optional)

START-TO-FINISH STEPS

1. Prepare clarified butter for scallops recipe (see pages 12–13). You will need 1 stick plus 2 tablespoons to yield ½ cup clarified butter.
2. While butter is melting, mince garlic for spinach recipe, mince shallot for sauce recipe, and slice shallots for salad recipe. Juice orange for sauce recipe and julienne rind, if using, for scallops recipe. Juice lemons for salad and for scallops.
3. Follow sauce recipe steps 1 through 3.
4. Follow salad recipe step 1 and spinach recipe step 1.
5. Follow salad recipe steps 2 and 3, and wipe out pan.
6. Follow scallops recipe steps 1 through 7.
7. Follow spinach recipe steps 2 and 3.
8. Follow salad recipe steps 4 and 5, scallops recipe steps 8 and 9, and serve.

RECIPES

Sautéed Scallops with White Wine Sauce

1½ pounds plump sea scallops
3 eggs
½ cup flour
½ cup clarified butter

½ cup olive oil
6 whole dried chili peppers
Juice of 1½ lemons
White wine sauce (see following recipe)
1 tablespoon julienned orange peel for garnish (optional)

1. In colander, rinse scallops under cold running water. Drain and pat dry with paper towels. Preheat oven to 200 degrees.
2. Separate eggs into 2 small bowls. Reserve whites for another use. Lightly whisk yolks with 2 tablespoons cold water.
3. Place flour on large flat plate.
4. Dip each scallop in yolks, let excess drip off, then roll in flour, coating evenly. Gently shake off excess flour.
5. In large sauté pan, heat ¼ cup clarified butter and ¼ cup olive oil over medium-high heat.
6. When butter-oil mixture is hot, add 3 chili peppers to pan. Cook, stirring with wooden spatula, until peppers begin to brown, 3 to 4 minutes. Using slotted spoon, remove peppers from pan and discard.
7. Add half the scallops to the pan and sauté until golden, about 3 minutes per side. With slotted spoon, transfer scallops to paper-towel-lined heatproof platter and keep warm in oven. Repeat with remaining chilies, adding more butter and oil as necessary, for second batch of scallops.
8. Remove scallops from oven and sprinkle with lemon juice.
9. Using slotted spoon, arrange a portion of scallops on each bed of spinach and top with sauce. Garnish with orange peel, if desired.

White Wine Sauce

¼ cup dry white wine
1 tablespoon dry sherry
1 tablespoon sherry vinegar
¼ cup fresh orange juice
2 teaspoons minced shallot
1 stick unsalted butter, chilled
Salt and freshly ground pepper

1. In medium-size non-aluminum saucepan, combine wine, sherry, vinegar, orange juice, and shallots. Bring to a boil over medium-high heat and reduce, stirring with wooden spoon, until about 2 tablespoons of syrupy liquid remain, 3 to 4 minutes. Reduce heat to very low.
2. Whisk in chilled butter, 1 tablespoon at a time. Season with salt and pepper to taste.
3. Pour sauce through sieve to remove shallot. Cover and keep warm over very low heat until ready to serve.

Spicy Spinach Sauté

1 pound spinach
⅓ cup olive oil
1 tablespoon minced garlic
¼ teaspoon Cayenne pepper, or ½ teaspoon red pepper flakes
Salt and freshly ground pepper

1. Stem spinach leaves. Rinse thoroughly under cold running water, drain in colander, and dry in salad spinner or pat dry with paper towels.
2. In large sauté pan, heat oil over medium-low heat. Add half the spinach leaves and turn heat to medium-high. Add half the garlic and cook, tossing with 2 wooden spoons, until oil begins to crackle, about 1 minute. Add 4 tablespoons water and toss. Add half the Cayenne pepper and salt and pepper to taste and continue to toss until spinach is wilted, 4 to 5 minutes. Transfer to sieve and press with back of spoon to extract excess liquid. Place in large heatproof bowl and keep warm in 200-degree oven. Repeat with remaining ingredients.
3. Divide among individual plates, forming bed for scallops.

Wild Mushroom Salad with Basil and Mint

2 cups arugula leaves
2 cups lamb's tongue, Boston, or other young lettuce leaves
¼ cup basil leaves
2 tablespoons mint leaves
⅔ pound fresh wild mushrooms, preferably chanterelles, shiitake, enokitake, or fresh cultivated mushrooms
1 cup olive oil
3 shallots, peeled and thinly sliced
Juice of 1 lemon
Salt and freshly ground pepper
2 tablespoons white wine vinegar

1. Rinse arugula, lamb's tongue, basil, and mint, and dry in salad spinner or pat dry with paper towels. Place in large bowl and set aside.
2. Wipe mushrooms clean with damp paper towels. With chef's knife, slice mushrooms into ¾-inch strips.
3. In large sauté pan, heat ½ cup oil over medium-high heat. Add mushrooms and sauté, stirring with wooden spatula, just until lightly browned, 4 to 5 minutes. Reduce heat to low, add shallots, and sauté just until tender. Stir in lemon juice and season mixture with salt and pepper to taste. Transfer mushroom mixture to bowl.
4. Using 2 wooden spoons, toss the salad greens with the remaining ½ cup oil and the vinegar. Season with salt and pepper to taste.
5. Divide greens among 4 dinner plates, arranging them on one side of plate, and top each bed of greens with a portion of mushrooms.

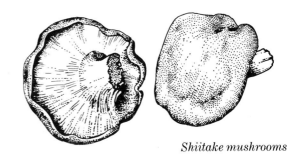

Shiitake mushrooms

Mussels and Shrimp in Coconut Cream with Mint
Stuffed Kohlrabi

For an attractive presentation, arrange the mussels and shrimp on a pinwheel of crisp snow peas and garnish each serving with a mussel shell. Serve the stuffed kohlrabi, sprinkled with minced thyme, on the side.

Thick coconut cream, blended with heavy cream, vermouth, and water, makes a sweet base for this unusual seafood combination. You can buy canned coconut cream in Oriental groceries and many supermarkets. Select snow peas that are very crisp and fresh-looking, and refrigerate them unwashed in a perforated plastic bag until you are ready to cook them. If fresh mint is not available, the cook recommends fresh basil or parsley. See page 11 for instructions on cleaning shrimp.

Kohlrabi, a member of the cabbage family, is a green bulb with long leafy stalks and slightly sweet, crunchy flesh. Select unblemished bulbs and refrigerate them in a perforated plastic bag. To hollow out the kohlrabi after cooking, first cool the bulb under cold running water and then, holding it in the palm of one hand, carve out the center with a sharp paring knife.

For the wild mushrooms, choose one from among the following: Golden-colored chanterelles, shaped like slender curved trumpets, are delicately flavored. Dark-brown shiitake mushrooms have velvety, thick caps with edges that are curled under when fresh. Enokitake resemble tiny, creamy-white umbrellas.

There is no substitute for kohlrabi for this recipe. If kohlrabi is unavailable, make the ADDED TOUCH salad of Jerusalem artichokes and Brussels sprouts.

WHAT TO DRINK

A full-bodied white wine is in order; try a Chardonnay or Pinot Blanc from California.

SHOPPING LIST AND STAPLES

3 pounds mussels
1 pound shrimp
4 small kohlrabi (about 1 pound total weight)
1 red bell pepper
½ pound snow peas
¼ pound fresh wild mushrooms, preferably chanterelles, shiitake, enokitake, or 2 ounces dried porcini (fresh cultivated may be substituted)
Medium-size Spanish onion (about ½ pound)
3 large or 6 small shallots
Small bunch mint
Small bunch thyme, preferably, or parsley
½ cup milk (if using homemade coconut cream)
½ pint heavy cream
1 tablespoon unsalted butter

18-ounce can cream of coconut
4 tablespoons virgin olive oil
6-ounce package shredded unsweetened coconut (if using homemade coconut cream)
Salt
Freshly ground black pepper
Freshly ground white pepper
1½ cups dry vermouth

UTENSILS

Food processor or blender (if using homemade coconut cream)
Stockpot with cover
Large deep skillet with cover or wide, low casserole with cover
Medium-size saucepan
Large sauté pan
Heatproof platter
Large bowl
Medium-size bowl (if using homemade coconut cream)
4 small bowls
Colander
Fine sieve (if using homemade coconut cream)
Measuring cups and spoons
Chef's knife
Paring knife
Slotted spoon
Wooden spoon
Wooden spatula
Melon baller (optional)
Stiff scrubbing brush
Cheesecloth or cloth napkin

START-TO-FINISH STEPS

One hour ahead: If preparing homemade coconut cream, combine ½ cup packaged shredded coconut with ½ cup boiling milk in medium-size bowl. Soak 20 to 30 minutes. Transfer to food processor or blender and process 4 to 5 minutes, or until smooth. Strain through a very fine sieve set over soaking bowl. With your hand, squeeze the pulp left in the sieve until you have extracted as much liquid as possible. Discard pulp and set aside liquid.

Fifteen to 20 minutes ahead: If using porcini for kohlrabi recipe, place in small bowl and soak in warm water to cover.

1. Follow mussels recipe steps 1 through 4.
2. While mussels are steaming, mince thyme for kohlrabi recipe and chop mint for mussels recipe. Follow mussels recipe step 5.
3. Follow kohlrabi recipe step 1.
4. While water is coming to a boil, follow kohlrabi recipe steps 2 through 5.
5. While kohlrabi are cooking, follow mussels recipe steps 6 through 8.
6. While poaching liquid is reducing, drain kohlrabi and follow recipe step 6.
7. Follow mussels recipe step 9 and kohlrabi recipe steps 7 through 10.
8. Follow mussels recipe steps 10 through 15.
9. Follow kohlrabi recipe step 11, mussels recipe step 16, and serve together.

RECIPES

Mussels and Shrimp in Coconut Cream with Mint

3 pounds mussels
1 pound shrimp
1½ cups dry vermouth
2 to 3 tablespoons cream of coconut, preferably homemade, or canned
1 cup heavy cream
2 large or 4 small shallots
1 tablespoon chopped fresh mint
Salt
½ pound snow peas
Fresh mint sprigs (optional)
Freshly ground white pepper

1. Scrub mussels well with stiff brush and remove beards.
2. Peel and devein shrimp.
3. In stockpot, bring vermouth and ¾ cup water to a boil. Reduce to a simmer.
4. Add mussels, cover, and cook, stirring occasionally, until they open, 4 to 5 minutes.
5. With slotted spoon, transfer mussels to large bowl, discarding any that have not opened.
6. In colander lined with triple thickness of cheesecloth or cloth napkin, strain mussel poaching liquid over deep skillet.
7. Shell mussels, reserving 2 or 3 shells per serving for garnish. Set mussels aside.

8. Over high heat, reduce mussel poaching liquid to about ¾ cup, about 10 minutes. Reduce heat to medium-high.
9. For sauce, add coconut cream and heavy cream to reduced poaching liquid. Stirring with wooden spoon, reduce by one-third, about 10 to 15 minutes.
10. Add shrimp and poach until they turn pink, about 3 minutes.
11. While shrimp are poaching, peel shallots and slice thinly.
12. Add mussels to sauce. Add shallots, chopped mint, and pepper to taste, and stir to combine. Remove skillet from heat, cover, and keep warm until ready to serve.
13. In saucepan used for kohlrabi, bring 1 quart salted water to a boil.
14. While water is coming to a boil, rinse snow peas under cold running water. Snap off ends and remove strings.
15. Add snow peas to boiling water, return water to a boil, and immediately pour snow peas into colander to drain. Refresh snow peas under cold running water and drain.
16. With slotted spoon, remove shrimp and mussels from sauce. Divide shrimp and mussels among 4 dinner plates. Top each portion with sauce and surround with "pinwheel" of snow peas. Arrange a few reserved mussel shells, open side down, near mussels and shrimp and garnish with fresh mint sprigs, if desired.

Stuffed Kohlrabi

1 red bell pepper
¼ pound fresh wild mushrooms, preferably chanterelles, shiitake, enokitake, or 2 ounces dried porcini, reconstituted (fresh cultivated may be substituted)
Medium-size Spanish onion (about ½ pound)
1 large or 2 small shallots
4 small kohlrabi (about 1 pound total weight)
4 tablespoons virgin olive oil
1 tablespoon unsalted butter
Salt
Freshly ground black pepper
½ teaspoon minced fresh thyme, preferably, or parsley

1. In medium-size saucepan, bring 1½ quarts water to a boil.
2. Core, seed, halve, and dice red pepper.
3. If using fresh mushrooms, wipe clean with damp paper towels and mince. If using porcini, drain, discard soaking liquid, pat dry, and mince.
4. Peel and dice onion. Peel and mince shallots.

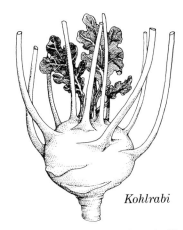

Kohlrabi

5. Trim kohlrabi and plunge into boiling water. Boil just until point of sharp knife pierces them easily, about 20 minutes. Drain in colander and dry pan.

6. Preheat oven to 200 degrees. In large sauté pan, heat 2 tablespoons oil over medium heat. Add red pepper and sauté until soft, 3 to 5 minutes. With slotted spoon, transfer to small bowl.

7. Add butter to pan. When butter has melted, add onion and sauté over medium heat until soft, about 5 minutes. With slotted spoon, transfer to another small bowl.

8. Add remaining 2 tablespoons oil to pan. Add mushrooms and shallots, and sauté over medium heat 3 to 4 minutes, or until shallots are translucent and mushrooms have softened slightly. With slotted spoon, transfer to third small bowl. Season each mixture wth salt and pepper to taste.

9. With paring knife, cut concentric circles in top of each kohlrabi, about 1 inch deep. With knife and melon baller, dig out and discard insides of kohlrabi to make shell about ¼ inch thick, taking caring not to break sides or puncture bottom.

10. Fill each shell with layers of pepper, onion, and mushroom-shallot mixture. Transfer to heatproof platter and keep warm in oven until ready to serve.

11. With chef's knife, carefully halve kohlrabis lengthwise. Sprinkle with minced thyme and serve.

ADDED TOUCH

Jerusalem artichokes, also known as sunchokes, can be peeled, but for the best flavor, use them unpeeled. This artichoke salad resembles a potato salad, and if Jerusalem artichokes are out of season, use potatoes instead.

Jerusalem Artichokes and Brussels Sprouts Salad

Salt
1 pound Brussels sprouts
1 pound small Jerusalem artichokes
½ red bell pepper
3 scallions
2 cloves garlic
½ cup virgin olive oil
1 tablespoon walnut pieces
Freshly ground pepper
2 tablespoons white wine vinegar flavored with tarragon or other herbs
1 tablespoon chopped flat-leaved parsley, preferably, or curly parsley

1. With paring knife, trim Brussels sprouts and Jerusalem artichokes.

2. In 2 medium-size covered saucepans, bring 1½ quarts water and 1½ teaspoons salt to a boil. Cook sprouts and artichokes until just tender, 20 to 25 minutes. Drain, separately, in colander.

3. Core, seed, and dice red pepper. Rinse scallions, pat dry with paper towels, and slice into ⅛-inch-thick rounds. Peel and mince garlic.

4. While sprouts are still warm, slice in half and place in medium-size bowl. Add ¼ cup oil, walnut pieces, and salt and pepper to taste, and toss.

5. While artichokes are still warm, cut into ¼-inch-thick slices, discarding any nubby ends. Do not peel. Place slices in medium-size bowl. Add red pepper, scallions, garlic, remaining ¼ cup oil, vinegar, parsley, and salt and pepper to taste and toss.

6. Arrange Brussels sprouts in center of salad platter and surround with Jerusalem artichokes.

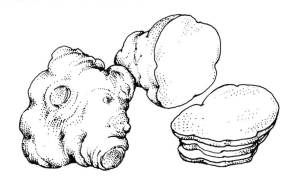

Jerusalem artichokes (sunchokes)

Clams in Sesame-Ginger Sauce
Fettuccine with Garlic and Oil
Mixed Vegetables, Oriental Style

This meal features two different Oriental-style recipes. The stir-fried clams, water chestnuts, and daikon are served on a bed of fettuccine and accompanied by a second stir-fry dish of snow peas, bean sprouts, and julienned vegetables.

Daikon, a crisp Japanese white radish, is available year-round in Oriental groceries and some supermarkets. Look for canned lychees in Oriental groceries or specialty food shops. Buy only an Oriental brand of sesame oil; the cold-pressed Middle Eastern variety is not a substitute.

WHAT TO DRINK

A California or Alsatian Gewürztraminer would match the spiciness in this menu; a Riesling would harmonize with the slight sweetness of the sauce.

SHOPPING LIST AND STAPLES

24 clams, preferably Cherrystone (about 3 pounds total weight)
½-pound Daikon, if available, or white radishes
½ pound snow peas
2 medium-size carrots (about ⅓ pound total weight)
Medium-size parsnip (about ¼ pound)
¼ pound bean sprouts
6 to 7 large cloves garlic
Medium-size leek (about ¼ pound)
Large bunch scallions
Small bunch fresh parsley
1½-inch piece fresh ginger
1 orange
1 egg
1 tablespoon unsalted butter
¼ pound Parmesan cheese
½ to ¾ pound fresh fettuccine, preferably, or dried
20-ounce can lychees
8-ounce can water chestnuts
½ cup plus 3½ tablespoons virgin olive oil
3 tablespoons Chinese sesame oil
3½ tablespoons soy sauce
1 tablespoon cornstarch
Salt and freshly ground pepper
¼ cup dry sherry

UTENSILS

Large stockpot with cover (if not using steamer unit)
Wok or large heavy-gauge skillet
Large saucepan
Steamer unit (optional)

Large heatproof bowl
2 small bowls
Colander
Measuring cups and spoons
Chef's knife
Paring knife
2 wooden spoons
Slotted spoon
Chinese wok spatulas (optional)
Grater
Wire scrub brush
Vegetable peeler

START-TO-FINISH STEPS

1. Follow clams recipe step 1.
2. Follow vegetables recipe steps 1 and 2.
3. Follow clams recipe step 2 and fettuccine recipe steps 1 and 2.
4. While pasta water is coming to a boil, follow vegetables recipe step 3 and clams recipe steps 3 through 6.
5. Follow fettuccine recipe steps 3 and 4, and vegetables recipe steps 4 and 5.
6. Follow fettuccine recipe step 5.
7. Follow clams recipe steps 7 through 10, vegetables recipe step 6, and serve.

RECIPES
Clams in Sesame-Ginger Sauce

24 clams, preferably Cherrystone
½-pound Daikon, if available, or white radishes
12 scallions
8-ounce can water chestnuts
20-ounce can lychees
1 tablespoon cornstarch
3 tablespoons Chinese sesame oil
1 tablespoon finely grated ginger
1 tablespoon minced garlic
¼ cup dry sherry
2 tablespoons soy sauce

1. Scrub clams and rinse thoroughly to rid them of sand. In large stockpot or steamer unit, bring ½ inch water to a boil. Add clams and steam, covered, 5 to 7 minutes.
2. With slotted spoon, transfer clams to colander.
3. When clams are cool enough to handle, remove from shells, discarding any that have not opened, and set aside. Reserve 2 or 3 shells per serving for garnish. Pour off cooking water, return clams to pot, cover, and keep warm.
4. Peel daikon and cut into 2 x ⅛-inch strips.
5. Rinse scallions and pat dry. Trim off root ends and most of green. Slit each scallion in half lengthwise.
6. Drain water chestnuts and lychees, and set aside. In small bowl, blend cornstarch with 1 tablespoon cold water.
7. Heat wok or skillet used for vegetables over medium-high heat for 30 seconds. Add oil. When hot, add Daikon, scallions, and water chestnuts, and stir fry 4 minutes.

8. Add ginger, garlic, sherry, soy sauce, and toss 1 minute. Add clams and lychees, and stir fry 1 minute.
9. Add cornstarch mixture to pan a few drops at a time, stirring constantly, until clam mixture reaches desired thickness. You may not need all the cornstarch.
10. Top each portion of fettuccine with a serving of clams and garnish with reserved clam shells.

Fettuccine with Garlic and Oil

Salt
½ cup plus 1 tablespoon virgin olive oil
1 egg
½ to ¾ pound fresh fettuccine, preferably, or dried
1 tablespoon finely minced garlic
¼ cup grated Parmesan cheese
1 tablespoon chopped parsley
Freshly ground pepper

1. Preheat oven to 200 degrees. In large covered saucepan, over high heat, bring 2 quarts water, 1 tablespoon salt, and 1 tablespoon olive oil to a boil.
2. In small bowl, beat egg with fork just until blended.
3. Add fettuccine to boiling water and cook 2 to 3 minutes for fresh, 8 to 12 minutes for dried, or just until *al dente*.
4. While pasta is cooking, warm 4 plates in oven.
5. Drain fettuccine in colander. Return hot pasta to pan. Add remaining ½ cup olive oil, and toss until evenly coated. Add egg, garlic, Parmesan, parsley, and salt and pepper to taste, and toss until combined. Divide among warmed plates and return to oven until ready to serve.

Mixed Vegetables, Oriental Style

½ pound snow peas
2 medium-size carrots (about ⅓ pound)
Medium-size parsnip (about ¼ pound)
Medium-size leek (about ¼ pound)
¼ pound bean sprouts, rinsed and drained
2½ tablespoons olive oil
2 teaspoons minced garlic
1½ tablespoons soy sauce
1 tablespoon grated orange peel
1 tablespoon unsalted butter

1. In colander, rinse snow peas, drain, and pat dry with paper towels. Pinch off stem ends and pull off strings.
2. Peel carrots and parsnip, and cut into ¼-inch-thick julienne strips.
3. Thoroughly rinse leek. Trim off root end and green part, and discard. With chef's knife, cut white part into ¼-inch-thick julienne strips.
4. Heat wok or large skillet over medium-high heat for 30 seconds. Add oil, tilting pan to coat surface evenly. When oil is hot, add the julienned vegetables and bean sprouts, and toss until well coated. Reduce heat to medium.
5. Add snow peas, garlic, and soy sauce, and stir fry just until vegetables are crisp-tender, 4 to 5 minutes. Turn into heatproof bowl and keep warm in oven. Wipe out pan.
6. Add orange peel and butter, and toss until blended.

Kathleen Kenny Sanderson

MENU 1 (Right)
Seafood Soup Provençale
Chèvre Florentine
Garlic Bread

MENU 2
Rainbow Trout
Julienned Vegetables
Saffron Rice Mold

MENU 3
Sea Bass with Fennel-Butter Sauce
Warm Potato Salad
Garden Salad with Mustard Vinaigrette

A s Kathleen Kenny Sanderson explains, "Most people are afraid of cooking with seafood because they do not understand how to handle it." But, in fact, preparing seafood should be a particular pleasure. In each of the menus here, the cook employs one of the standard French techniques—she poaches the fish and shellfish in Menu 1, sautés the trout in Menu 2, and both poaches and bakes the sea bass in Menu 3—then improvises to make each recipe her own. Consequently, all her menus have French overtones, even if she uses American products. If you cook all three of these menus, you will have mastered three essential techniques of fish cookery.

The fish stew of Menu 1 resembles the classic bouillabaisse of the Mediterranean city Marseilles. However, this version uses only four kinds of fish and shellfish rather than the traditional variety of twelve or more. The trout of Menu 2, served with lemon juice, butter, and parsley, is served with saffron rice rather than the more typical French accompaniment, boiled potatoes. For Menu 3, the sea bass, served with a fresh fennel-butter sauce, is accompanied by a garden salad of four distinctive greens.

Seafood soup provençale makes an impressive main-course offering for this informal meal. Serve the spinach salad with goat cheese and a chunk of garlic bread on the same plate. Offer guests extra bread in a napkin-lined basket.

Seafood Soup Provençale
Chèvre Florentine
Garlic Bread

Kathleen Kenny Sanderson uses two varieties each of shellfish and fish for her substantial stew—a perfect cold-weather company meal. Of these, goosefish is probably the least familiar. The only edible section of the fish is the tail section, which contains a firm lobster-like meat. You can use sea bass in its place, and then select either cod or halibut for your other fish. Or use any combination you like, according to what is fresh in your market. Just be sure to use a firm, white-fleshed fish. You can also use frozen fish if you thaw it partially before adding it to the soup. This way it will not overcook and fall apart.

Pernod is often used in bouillabaisse because its delicate anise flavor enhances seafood. This yellowish French liqueur is sold in well-stocked liquor stores.

Chèvre Florentine, a goat's cheese and spinach salad, is unusual and simple to prepare. Chèvre is a generic name for goat's cheese, and Montrachet, a moderately mild variety, is shaped like a log and sometimes coated with a thin layer of edible black ash. Substitute any other goat cheese, or feta, if Montrachet is unavailable.

WHAT TO DRINK

A crisp, dry white wine like an Italian Verdicchio is the best selection, or choose a French Muscadet.

SHOPPING LIST AND STAPLES

½ pound fillet of cod, halibut, or sea bass, cut 1 inch thick
½ pound fillet of goosefish (also known as monkfish and angler fish)
12 littleneck clams or mussels
12 medium-size shrimp
1 pound spinach
3 large carrots
1 bunch celery
Medium-size red bell pepper
Large yellow onion
4 cloves garlic,
2 shallots
Small bunch fresh basil, or 1 teaspoon dried
Small bunch fresh oregano, or 1 teaspoon dried
1 stick unsalted butter
½ pound chèvre, preferably Montrachet, or feta cheese
16-ounce can Italian plum tomatoes
¾ cup virgin olive oil
3 tablespoons white wine vinegar
1 loaf French or Italian bread, white or whole wheat

½ teaspoon crushed red pepper
1 bay leaf
Salt and freshly ground pepper
¾ cup dry white wine
2 tablespoons Pernod

UTENSILS

Large saucepan
Small saucepan
15½ x 12-inch cookie sheet
Plate
Salad bowl
2 small bowls
Salad spinner (optional)
Measuring cups and spoons
Chef's knife
Paring knife
Ladle
Wooden spoon
Stiff scrubbing brush
Vegetable peeler (optional)

START-TO-FINISH STEPS

1. For garlic bread recipe, remove butter from refrigerator.
2. Follow chèvre recipe steps 1 through 3.
3. Follow soup recipe steps 1 through 5. While vegetables are cooking, follow garlic bread recipe steps 1 and 2.
4. Follow soup recipe step 6. While soup is cooking, follow garlic bread recipe steps 3 and 4.
5. Follow soup recipe step 7 and chèvre recipe steps 4 through 6.
6. Follow soup recipe step 8 and chèvre recipe step 7.
7. Follow soup recipe step 9.
8. While fish is cooking follow chèvre recipe step 8 and garlic bread recipe step 5.
9. Follow chèvre recipe step 9, soup recipe step 10, and serve with garlic bread.

RECIPES

Seafood Soup Provençale

3 large carrots
Large yellow onion
2 stalks celery

12 medium-size shrimp
12 littleneck clams or mussels
½ pound fillet of goosefish (also known as monkfish and angler-fish)
½ pound fillet of cod, halibut, or sea bass, cut 1 inch thick
¼ cup virgin olive oil
¾ cup dry white wine
2 tablespoons Pernod
16-ounce can Italian plum tomatoes
1 bay leaf
Salt and freshly ground pepper

1. Peel carrots and onion and wash celery. Cut carrots, celery, and onion into ¼-inch slices. Cut through onion rings crosswise to separate them into semi-circles.
2. Shell and devein shrimp (see page 11).
3. With stiff scrubbing brush, scrub clams or mussels under cold running water. Debeard mussels if necessary. Rinse thoroughly and discard any that have open shells.
4. Wipe goosefish and cod with damp paper towels. With chef's knife, cut fish into 1½-inch squares.
5. In large saucepan, heat oil over medium-high heat. Reduce heat to medium. Add carrots, onion, and celery, and sauté, stirring with wooden spoon, until carrots and celery are bright in color, 2 to 3 minutes.
6. Add wine and Pernod, and cook over medium-high heat 2 to 3 minutes.
7. Add tomatoes with their juice, bay leaf, and salt and pepper to taste. Bring to a boil over medium-high heat, then reduce to a simmer and cook, uncovered, 4 to 5 minutes.
8. Add shrimp and clams or mussels, and simmer 3 minutes.
9. Add fish and simmer just until firm, about 5 minutes.
10. Remove bay leaf and ladle soup into 4 individual bowls. Place bowls on dinner plates and serve.

Chèvre Florentine

2 cloves garlic
½ cup virgin olive oil
½ teaspoon crushed red pepper
½ pound chèvre, preferably Montrachet, or feta cheese
1 pound spinach
Medium-size red bell pepper
2 shallots
3 tablespoons white wine vinegar

1. Pell garlic and mince finely.
2. In small saucepan, combine oil, garlic, and crushed red pepper, and sauté over medium heat just until garlic turns golden brown, about 2 minutes.
3. Slice chèvre evenly into 8 rounds or break feta into 8 pieces and place cheese on plate. Transfer 5 tablespoons oil to small bowl and spoon remaining oil, with garlic and red pepper, over chèvre. Set aside.
4. Wash spinach and remove and discard stems. Dry spinach in salad spinner or pat dry with paper towels.
5. Wash red bell pepper and pat dry with paper towels.

Core, halve, and seed pepper. Cut into ½-inch dice and set aside.
6. Peel and mince shallots.
7. In salad bowl, combine spinach, red pepper, and shallots.
8. Toss salad with reserved oil and then with vinegar.
9. Divide salad among 4 dinner plates, arranging on one-third of each plate, and top each serving with 2 slices marinated chèvre.

Garlic Bread

2 cloves garlic
1 stick unsalted butter, at room temperature
1 tablespoon minced fresh basil, or 1 teaspoon dried
1 tablespoon minced fresh oregano, or 1 teaspoon dried
½ teaspoon freshly ground pepper
1 loaf French or Italian bread, white or whole wheat

1. Preheat broiler.
2. Peel garlic and mince finely.
3. In small bowl, mash together butter, garlic, basil, oregano, and pepper until thoroughly combined.
4. Halve bread lengthwise and spread cut sides with butter mixture. Place on cookie sheet, buttered sides up.
5. Broil bread until butter is brown and bubbly and bread is lightly toasted, 1 to 2 minutes.

ADDED TOUCH

Sabayon is a sweet egg-custard sauce that can be served warm over fruit or eaten on its own.

Strawberries and White Wine Sabayon

2½ cups strawberries or raspberries
6 eggs
⅓ cup sugar
⅓ cup dry white wine
1 cup heavy cream, well-chilled
2 tablespoons Grand Marnier

1. In colander, rinse berries under cold running water and drain. Gently pat dry with paper towels. Hull, if necessary, and set aside.
2. Using 2 small bowls, separate eggs, reserving whites for another use, and set aside yolks.
3. In bottom of double boiler, over high heat, bring just enough water to a boil so that water level will be ½-inch below bottom of upper half of double boiler.
4. In upper half of double boiler, combine egg yolks and sugar, and whisk until pale yellow and creamy.
5. Add wine to egg yolk mixture and place top half of double boiler over simmering water in bottom half. Taking care that water never boils, whisk mixture constantly until thickened into fluffy custard, about 5 minutes.
6. Remove mixture from heat and continue whisking until cool.
7. In small stainless steel bowl, whip cream until stiff.
8. With rubber spatula, fold whipped cream into egg yolk mixture. Gently fold in liqueur. Spoon over berries.

Rainbow Trout
Julienned Vegetables
Saffron Rice Mold

Garnish the fish with parsley sprigs and halved lemon "wheels." Colorful saffron rice and julienned vegetables accompany the fish.

Fresh rainbow trout is a delicacy and is at its best when just caught. Tank-bred trout are sold live in specialty food shops and good fish markets. Store fresh trout packed in ice in the refrigerator until you are ready to cook it. Frozen trout is commonly available but may have lost some of its delicate flavor. Defrost frozen trout overnight in the refrigerator.

WHAT TO DRINK

A good-quality white Burgundy, such as a Meursault, or a fine California Chardonnay are right for this trout classic.

SHOPPING LIST AND STAPLES

4 whole rainbow trout, bluefish, or perch (8 to 10 ounces each), or eight ½-inch thick fillets (3 to 4 ounces each)
½ pound carrots
½ pound yellow squash
½ pound zucchini
Large red bell pepper (optional)
1 bunch scallions
Medium-size bunch fresh parsley
Small bunch fresh dill, or 1 teaspoon dried
2 lemons

1 stick plus 2 tablespoons unsalted butter
2¼ cups chicken stock, preferably homemade
 (see page 13), or canned
¼ cup plus 1 tablespoon vegetable oil
1 cup long-grain rice
⅓ to ½ cup flour
½ to 1 teaspoon saffron threads
Salt and freshly ground pepper
⅓ cup dry white wine

UTENSILS

2 large skillets
Medium-size sauté pan with cover
Small saucepan
Four ½-cup ramekins or custard cups
Large plate
Measuring cups and spoons
Chef's knife
Paring knife
Wooden spoon
Wooden spatula
Whisk
Vegetable peeler
Mortar and pestle

START-TO-FINISH STEPS

1. Follow rice recipe steps 1 through 5.
2. While rice is cooking, wash, dry, and chop parsley for trout and rice recipes, and follow trout recipe steps 1 through 5.
3. While first batch of trout is cooking, follow vegetables recipe step 1 and rice recipe step 6.
4. Follow trout recipe step 6.
5. Follow rice recipe step 7 and, after turning trout, vegetables recipe steps 2 and 3.
6. Follow trout recipe steps 7 through 9, rice recipe step 8, and serve with vegetables.

RECIPES

Rainbow Trout

2 lemons
4 whole rainbow trout, bluefish, or perch (8 to 10 ounces
 each), or eight ½-inch-thick fillets (3 to 4 ounces each)
⅓ to ½ cup flour
Salt and freshly ground pepper
¼ cup vegetable oil
⅓ cup dry white wine
⅓ cup chopped parsley, plus additional sprigs for garnish
1 stick unsalted butter

1. Preheat oven to 200 degrees.
2. Squeeze enough lemon to measure ⅓ cup juice and slice lemon "wheels" for garnish.
3. If using whole fish, remove fins and, with knife, gently scrape skin to remove scales. Wipe whole fish or fillets with damp paper towels and pat dry.
4. On large flat plate, mix flour with salt and pepper to taste. Roll fish or dip fillets in flour to coat lightly.
5. In large skillet, heat 2 tablespoons oil over medium-high heat. Add 2 whole fish or 4 fillets. Cook whole fish 4 minutes per side, fillets 2 to 3 minutes per side, turning with spatula. Transfer to plates and place in oven.
6. Repeat cooking process with remaining fish.
7. Pour off excess oil. Add lemon juice, wine, and ⅓ cup parsley to skillet. Over medium-high heat, reduce liquid by about half, about 3 minutes.
8. Add butter, 1 tablespoon at a time, whisking constantly.
9. Remove plates from oven, pour sauce over fish, and garnish with parsley sprigs and halved lemon "wheels."

Julienned Vegetables

½ pound carrots, peeled
½ pound yellow squash
½ pound zucchini
Large red bell pepper, cored and seeded (optional)
2 tablespoons unsalted butter
¼ cup chicken stock
1 tablespoon chopped fresh dill, or 1 teaspoon dried
Salt and freshly ground pepper

1. With chef's knife, julienne all vegetables, cutting into 3-inch matchsticks.
2. In large skillet, melt butter over medium heat. Add vegetables and toss with wooden spatula until completely coated with butter. Add chicken stock and dill, and cook over medium-high heat, stirring, until just crisp tender, 2 to 3 minutes. Season with salt and pepper to taste.
3. Keep warm over very low heat.

Saffron Rice Mold

1 bunch scallions
2 cups chicken stock
½ to 1 teaspoon loosely packed saffron threads
1 tablespoon vegetable oil
1 cup long-grain rice
Salt and freshly ground pepper
1 tablespoon chopped parsley (optional)

1. Wash scallions and pat dry with paper towels. Trim scallions and dice enough to measure ½ cup.
2. In small saucepan, bring chicken stock to a boil over medium-high heat.
3. With mortar and pestle, pulverize saffron threads.
4. In medium-size sauté pan, heat oil over medium-high heat. Add scallions and sauté 1 minute. Add rice and saffron, and sauté, stirring, 1 minute.
5. Add boiling stock to rice mixture and add salt and pepper to taste. Return to a boil over medium-high heat, then reduce to a simmer. Cover and cook 18 minutes.
6. Turn off heat. Let sit 10 minutes.
7. Lightly butter four ½-cup ramekins or custard cups.
8. Pack rice into ramekins, and then invert and unmold onto plates. Garnish with parsley, if desired.

Sea Bass with Fennel-Butter Sauce
Warm Potato Salad
Garden Salad with Mustard Vinaigrette

You can serve sea bass with the skin on, but the cook suggests that you skin it before eating, although the skin is edible. The butter sauce contains chopped fresh fennel, also know as *finocchio*. Fennel has a bulbous base and feathery green leaves. Select bulbs that are firm and have no soft or brownish spots. Fennel is sold in Italian groceries or well-stocked supermarkets during fall and winter. If fresh fennel is unavailable, substitute fennel or anise seeds and crush them to release their flavor.

A warm potato salad and a chilled garden salad accom-

Silvery sea bass topped with fennel-butter sauce and garnished with a sprig of watercress makes an elegant company dish. Serve the potato salad with the fish, and the garden salad separately.

pany the sea bass. For the warm salad, select evenly sized new red potatoes for uniform cooking. Be sure they are firm and have smooth unblemished skins. Pour the dressing on while the potatoes are still warm so that it soaks in.

The garden salad combines four leafy vegetables, watercress, radicchio, arugula, and endive, with contrasting colors and textures. Watercress should be crisp and bright green, and is available all year. Radicchio, an Italian wild chicory, has ruby red leaves, is shaped like a small head of lettuce, and is tightly packed like cabbage. You can buy it only at quality greengrocers, usually during the winter. Arugula, a popular Italian salad green, has long slender notched leaves that should look crisp and not wilted or discolored. Arugula is often sandy and must be rinsed thoroughly before use. Belgian endive grows in a compact

head consisting of long slender white leaves with pale yellow tips. All salad greens should be wrapped in plastic bags and refrigerated.

WHAT TO DRINK

A firm, acidic wine is what this menu calls for, and there are several candidates: a California Sauvignon Blanc, a small-château Graves from Bordeaux, a Pouilly Fumé from the Loire, or an Italian Greco di Tufo.

SHOPPING LIST AND STAPLES

4 fillets of sea bass, sea trout, or halibut (each about 8 ounces), with or without skin

1½ pounds new red potatoes
Medium-size fennel bulb, or 1 tablespoon fennel seeds or anise seeds
1 head radicchio or small head escarole
1 head endive
Small bunch arugula
Medium-size bunch watercress
1 bunch scallions
Medium-size bunch parsley
1 bunch chives (optional)
1 lemon
1 egg
2 sticks plus 1 tablespoon unsalted butter, approximately
1⅓ cups vegetable oil
¼ cup red wine vinegar or balsamic vinegar

1 tablespoon whole-grain mustard
Dash of Worcestershire sauce
Salt
Freshly ground pepper
2½ cups dry white wine

UTENSILS

2 medium-size saucepans with covers
7 x 12-inch flameproof baking dish
Metal steamer
3 small bowls
Colander
Salad spinner (optional)
Measuring cups and spoons
Chef's knife
Paring knife
Wooden spoon
Metal spatula
Juicer (optional)
2 whisks

START-TO-FINISH STEPS

1. Follow potato salad recipe steps 1 through 3.
2. While potatoes are boiling, follow fennel-butter sauce recipe steps 1 and 2.
3. While wine is reducing, follow garden salad recipe steps 1 through 4 and sea bass recipe step 1.
4. Follow fennel-butter sauce recipe step 3 and potato salad recipe step 4.
5. Follow sea bass recipe steps 2 through 5.
6. While fish is baking, follow garden salad recipe steps 5 through 7 and potato salad recipe step 5.
7. Follow fennel-butter sauce recipe step 4, sea bass recipe steps 6 and 7, garden salad recipe step 8, potato salad recipe step 6, and serve.

RECIPES

Sea Bass with Fennel-Butter Sauce

4 fillets of sea bass, sea trout, or halibut (each about 8 ounces), with or without skin
1 tablespoon unsalted butter, approximately
½ cup dry white wine
Salt
Freshly ground pepper

Fennel-butter sauce (see following recipe)
Watercress sprigs for garnish (optional)

1. Preheat oven to 400 degrees.
2. Wipe fish with damp paper towels.
3. Butter flameproof 7 x 12-inch baking dish.
4. In baking dish, bring ½ cup water and wine to a boil over medium-high heat. Add fish and salt and pepper to taste, and cover tightly with aluminum foil.
5. Bake until fish flakes easily when tested with fork, 5 to 6 minutes.
6. While fish is baking, warm dinner plates under hot running water and dry.
7. With metal spatula, transfer fillets to warm dinner plates. Top with fennel-butter sauce and garnish with watercress sprigs, if desired. Skin fillets before eating, if desired.

Fennel-Butter Sauce

Medium-size fennel bulb, or 1 tablespoon fennel seeds or anise seeds
½ bunch scallions
1½ cups dry white wine
2 sticks unsalted butter

1. Rinse fennel, trim off ends and feathery greens, and dice enough of bulb to measure 1 cup. Rinse and trim scallions and finely chop enough to measure ⅓ cup.
2. In medium-size saucepan, combine fennel, scallions, and wine, and bring to a boil over high heat. Lower heat to medium-high and reduce liquid until wine is almost evaporated, 8 to 10 minutes, taking care that vegetables do not singe.
3. Reduce heat to very low, and whisk in butter, 1 tablespoon at a time, until completely incorporated. Cover pan partially and turn off heat, but leave pan on burner until ready to serve.
4. Whisk sauce to recombine.

Warm Potato Salad

1½ pounds new red potatoes
1 lemon
⅓ cup chopped parsley
¼ cup finely chopped chives or scallion greens
⅓ cup vegetable oil
Salt
Freshly ground pepper

1. Wash potatoes, but do not peel.
2. In medium-size saucepan fitted with steamer, bring 2 inches water to a boil. Place potatoes in steamer, cover, and steam just until potatoes can be easily penetrated with tip of sharp knife, 15 to 20 minutes, depending on size of potatoes.
3. Squeeze enough lemon to measure 2 tablespoons juice. Wash parsley and chives or scallions and pat dry. Chop enough parsley to measure ⅓ cup. Trim chives or scallion greens, and finely chop enough to measure ¼ cup.
4. Drain potatoes in colander and return to pan off heat.
5. In small bowl, combine parsley, chives, and lemon juice. Add oil, salt and pepper to taste, and whisk until blended. Set aside.
6. Slice potatoes and arrange on dinner plates alongside fish. Spoon dressing over warm potatoes.

Garden Salad with Mustard Vinaigrette

1 head radicchio or small head escarole
Medium-size bunch watercress
Small bunch arugula
1 head endive
1 egg
1 tablespoon whole-grain mustard
¼ cup red wine vinegar or balsamic vinegar
Dash of Worcestershire sauce
1 cup vegetable oil
Salt
Freshly ground pepper

1. Place salad bowls in freezer to chill.
2. Separate radicchio leaves and discard core. Remove stems from watercress. Trim arugula stems. Wash radicchio, watercress, and arugula, and dry in salad spinner or pat dry with paper towels.
3. Remove bruised outer leaves of endive. Slice ½ inch off base of endive, then slice endive in half crosswise and lengthwise, and separate leaves.
4. Remove salad bowls from freezer and divide greens among them. Cover and refrigerate until ready to serve.
5. Separate egg, placing yolk in small bowl and reserving white for another use. Whisk yolk until thick and lemon-colored, 1 to 2 minutes. Beating constantly, add oil in thin stream until completely incorporated.
6. In another small bowl, combine mustard, vinegar, and Worcestershire sauce, and stir until blended.
7. Slowly drizzle mustard mixture into egg mixture, whisk-

ing constantly. Season with salt and pepper to taste. Set aside.
8. Toss salad with mustard vinaigrette and serve.

ADDED TOUCH

Bosc pears are ideal for poaching, as in this recipe, and will soak up the color of the red wine. For a more intense flavor, prepare the pears a day in advance and let them steep in the wine overnight.

Spiced Pears in Red Wine

2 cups red wine
2 cups sugar
2 whole cloves
1 cinnamon stick, 1½ to 2 inches long
½ teaspoon grated lemon peel
½ teaspoon grated orange peel
4 Bosc pears (4 to 5 ounces each)
1 tablespoon cornstarch
4 mint sprigs for garnish (optional)

1. In medium-size saucepan, combine wine, sugar, cloves, cinnamon stick, and lemon and orange peels. Bring to a boil over high heat, then cover and reduce to a simmer.
2. Peel pears, leaving stems intact. Stand pears upright in wine, stem side up. If necessary, add water so that liquid barely covers pears.
3. Cover pan and poach pears until tender, 20 to 25 minutes.
4. Remove from heat. Uncover and allow pears to cool in liquid. With slotted spoon, transfer pears to dessert plates.
5. Bring wine mixture to a boil over medium-high heat and boil until reduced to 1 cup, 8 to 10 minutes.
6. In small bowl, mix cornstarch with ¾ cup cold water. In a slow, steady stream, add boiling wine, whisking until incorporated. Lower heat to medium-high and stir sauce until thick enough to coat spoon, 2 to 3 minutes.
7. Pour sauce through fine sieve set over bowl and let cool.
8. When sauce has cooled, pour ¼ cup around each pear, and garnish each serving with a mint sprig if desired.

LEFTOVER SUGGESTION

Use leftover raw fennel by chopping it up and adding it to salads, meat balls, or meat loaf. Or, braise the fennel and serve it with poultry or veal.

Mark Miller

MENU 1 (Left)
Spicy Squid Salad
Broiled Tuna with Orange-Cumin Sauce
Sauté of Squash, Onions, and Peppers

MENU 2
Oyster Seviche
Baked Red Snapper with Chili Sauce
Green Rice

MENU 3
Salmon à la Tartare
Poached Oysters with Saffron-Cream Sauce

Californian Mark Miller learned to love the foods of Southeast Asia, Latin America, and Africa while a graduate student in anthropology: "I attempt to bridge two worlds by using classic French techniques to re-create these cuisines," he says. "And I strive to maintain the integrity of each cuisine." He admires the way ethnic cooks use vibrant flavors and colors, as typified by the Yucatán cooking he most often emulates. Influenced by their Mayan forbears, Yucatán cooks season their meals with limes, garlic, and roasted chilies—all ingredients Mark Miller loves—to produce a richly textured, peppery cuisine. Both Menu 1 and Menu 2 are Yucatán-inspired meals. The spicy squid salad and broiled tuna of Menu 1 call for hot jalapeño peppers, coriander, garlic, lime juice, and cumin, all ubiquitous Latin seasonings. In Menu 2, the oyster appetizer is *seviche*, a raw-fish recipe devised by Peruvians and now a universal favorite in Latin America. Although white-fleshed fish is now the usual main ingredient, shellfish is sometimes used. The fish or shellfish "cook" in the lime- and lemon-juice marinade. To spice the *seviche*, the cook adds diced California green chilies and minced jalapeño and serrano peppers. The red snapper entrée is served with a highly seasoned sauce of orange, lemon, and lime juices, *achiote* seeds, and three kinds of chili powder.

For a change of pace, in Menu 3 Mark Miller serves salmon à la tartare on toasted slices of bread, accompanied by poached oysters and spinach on pasta tossed with a vivid saffron sauce.

A marinated spicy squid salad precedes the main course of broiled tuna steaks topped with an orange-cumin sauce and the side dish of sautéed vegetables. Orange slices and parsley sprigs are an optional garnish.

Spicy Squid Salad
Broiled Tuna with Orange-Cumin Sauce
Sauté of Squash, Onions, and Peppers

Rather than a traditional butter and cream mixture, Mark Miller uses fresh orange juice, flavored with cumin and brown sugar, in the basting sauce for the broiled tuna steaks. Cumin, an essential flavoring ingredient in Mexican recipes, has a pungent taste.

For the first-course salad, the squid is blanched very quickly and then marinated in a spicy mixture of oil, vinegar, lime juice, onion, garlic, fresh coriander (also known as Chinese parsley), and fresh jalapeño peppers. Small hot jalapeño peppers may be available fresh only in Latin groceries and supermarkets that stock exotic ingredients. You may want to buy enough for Menu 2; otherwise, canned pickled serranos are acceptable substitutes. As with all hot chilies, be sure to wear rubber gloves when handling them and avoid touching your eyes or face.

WHAT TO DRINK

A dry white wine can act as a foil for the complex flavors here. A Muscadet from France or a Verdicchio from Italy would do well.

SHOPPING LIST AND STAPLES

Four ¾-inch-thick fillets of bluefin tuna, yellowtail, or mackerel (each about 8 ounces)
1 pound cleaned squid (about 3 squid)
2 ripe tomatoes, preferably beefsteak
1 pound very young yellow squash
1 pound very young zucchini
Medium-size red bell pepper
2 fresh jalapeño peppers, preferably, or 2 fresh serrano peppers or 3-ounce can serranos
2 medium-size red onions
3 large cloves garlic
Small bunch parsley (optional)
1 bunch coriander
3 juice oranges plus 1 orange (optional)
2 large limes
1 lemon
1 tablespoon unsalted butter
1¼ cups virgin olive oil
¼ cup rice wine vinegar
1 tablespoon dark brown sugar
¼ cup cumin seeds
Salt
Freshly ground pepper

UTENSILS

Stockpot or large saucepan
Small heavy-gauge skillet
Large sauté pan
Small saucepan
Broiling pan
Large stainless steel or glass bowl
Colander
Measuring cups and spoons
Chef's knife
Paring knife
Wooden spoon
Metal spatula
Wooden spatula
Juicer
Mortar and pestle (optional)
Rolling pin (if not using mortar and pestle)
Pastry brush

START-TO-FINISH STEPS

1. Follow squid recipe step 1. While water is coming to a boil, prepare vegetables and herbs for squid and squash recipes. Be sure to wear thin rubber gloves when handling jalapeño peppers. Squeeze citrus juices for squid, tuna, and squash recipes.
2. Follow squid recipe steps 2 through 4.
3. Follow tuna recipe steps 1 through 3.
4. Follow squid recipe step 5 and serve.
5. Follow tuna recipe steps 4 and 5. While broiling tuna on first side, follow squash recipe step 1.
6. Turn fillets, follow tuna recipe step 6 and squash recipe step 2.
7. Follow tuna recipe step 7, squash recipe step 3, and serve.

RECIPES

Spicy Squid Salad

2 tablespoons salt
1 pound cleaned squid (about 3 squid)
2 tomatoes, preferably beefsteak, quartered
¾ cup diced red onion
2 tablespoons diced fresh jalapeño or serrano peppers (with seeds), or 2 tablespoons diced canned serranos, with seeds

½ cup chopped fresh coriander leaves
1 teaspoon minced garlic
¾ cup virgin olive oil
¼ cup rice wine vinegar
¼ cup fresh lime juice

1. In stockpot or in large saucepan, bring 4 quarts water and salt to a boil. Place serving bowl in freezer to chill.
2. Slice cleaned squid into ¼-to ⅓-inch-thick rings. Add squid to boiling water and blanch 30 seconds.
3. In colander, drain squid and immediately refresh under cold running water.
4. Shake colander to remove excess water and turn squid into large stainless steel or glass bowl. Add remaining ingredients and toss to combine. Cover with plastic wrap and chill until ready to serve.
5. Remove squid from refrigerator and turn into serving bowl.

Broiled Tuna with Orange-Cumin Sauce

¼ cup cumin seeds
1 cup fresh orange juice
1 tablespoon dark brown sugar
Four ¾-inch-thick fillets of bluefin tuna, yellowtail, or
    mackerel
¼ cup virgin olive oil
1 orange, thinly sliced, for garnish (optional)
Parsley sprigs for garnish (optional)

1. In small dry heavy-gauge skillet, toast cumin seeds over medium heat about 2 minutes, or until fragrance is released. Shake skillet from time to time to keep seeds from scorching. Grind seeds with mortar and pestle or place between 2 sheets of wax paper and crush with rolling pin.
2. For sauce, combine juice, cumin, and sugar in small saucepan. Bring to a boil over high heat and reduce sauce to ½ cup, about 5 minutes.
3. Preheat broiler.
4. Wipe tuna fillets with damp paper towels. Place fillets in broiling pan and brush them on both sides with olive oil.
5. Broil 4 to 5 inches from heating element, 3 to 4 minutes per side.
6. While fillets are broiling, warm serving platter under hot running water.
7. Just before fillets are done, dry platter. With metal spatula, transfer fillets to warm platter and top each with

sauce. Garnish platter with orange slices and parsley sprigs, if desired.

Sauté of Squash, Onions, and Peppers

¼ cup virgin olive oil
1 cup thinly sliced red onion crescents
1 cup julienned red bell pepper
1 cup ¼-inch-thick slices very young yellow squash
1 cup ¼-inch-thick slices very young zucchini
1 tablespoon minced garlic
½ teaspoon salt
¼ teaspoon freshly ground pepper
¼ teaspoon lemon juice, approximately
1 tablespoon unsalted butter

1. In large sauté pan, heat oil over medium-low heat. Add onion and red bell pepper, and sauté about 4 minutes or until wilted. Be careful not to let onions brown.
2. Add squash, zucchini, garlic, salt, and pepper, and stir to combine. Add lemon juice by drops, being careful not to add too much—lemon flavor should not be discernable in dish. Stirring with wooden spatula, sauté squash 2 minutes, or just until squash begins to soften.
3. Remove pan from heat, add butter, and toss. Turn into serving bowl.

ADDED TOUCH

For this summery dessert, cantaloupe balls and blackberries are soaked in a fruit-flavored liqueur such as Chambord, Crème de Cassis, or Cherry Heering. If you prefer, you can use another melon and berry combination.

Cantaloupe and Blackberry Compote

1 cantaloupe (about 2 pounds) or other melon
½ pound fresh blackberries, or other berries
3 tablespoons fruit liqueur (Chambord, Crème de Cassis,
    or Cherry Heering)
4 fresh mint sprigs

1. Cut cantaloupe in half and remove seeds with spoon. With melon baller, cut flesh into balls.
2. In colander, rinse blackberries under cold running water and drain. Gently pat dry with paper towels.
3. Place melon balls and berries in large bowl. Sprinkle fruit with liqueur and toss. Cover and refrigerate 1 hour.
4. Divide fruit among 4 sherbet glasses and garnish each serving with mint sprig.

Oyster Seviche
Baked Red Snapper with Chili Sauce
Green Rice

Offer your guests the oyster seviche as an appetizer while the red snapper bakes. Serve the green rice to one side of the fish, and garnish each plate with lime wedges and orange slices, if desired.

The prologue to this peppery meal is a colorful oyster seviche. For a flavor accent, Mark Miller uses two types of chilies: jalapeño and serrano.

The red-snapper sauce contains ground *achiote* seeds, which are also sold under the name "annatto." In addition, the sauce calls for three different varieties of chili powder—ancho, New Mexico, and California. If you cannot find all three, use 10 tablespoons of just one of them. You can substitute commercially blended chili powder, but only if it contains no sugar, starch, or other seasonings.

WHAT TO DRINK

Because of the Mexican flavorings, this menu is more compatible with cold beer or light ale than with wine.

SHOPPING LIST AND STAPLES

24 extra-small shucked oysters with liquor
Four ¾-inch-thick fillets of red snapper or any white, meaty fish, such as tilefish, grouper, halibut, or scrod (each about 8 ounces)
Small head Romaine lettuce
Medium-size red bell pepper
2 California green chilies, approximately
2 fresh jalapeño peppers, or 7-ounce can
1 fresh serrano pepper, or 3-ounce can
2 medium-sized shallots
2 large cloves garlic
2 medium-size bunches fresh coriander
6 oranges, preferably undyed Valencias
5 limes
1 lemon
1 tablespoon unsalted butter
⅓ cup plus 2 tablespoons virgin olive oil
1 tablespoon rice wine vinegar
1 cup long-grain white rice
4 tablespoons ancho chili powder
3 tablespoons New Mexico chili powder
3 tablespoons California chili powder
1 teaspoon dried *achiote* seeds
Dash of Cayenne pepper
Salt and freshly ground black pepper

UTENSILS

Food processor or blender
Medium-size heavy-gauge saucepan with cover

Small saucepan
13 x 9 x 2-inch baking pan
Large stainless steel bowl
Salad spinner (optional)
Measuring cups and spoons
Chef's knife
Paring knife
Large stainless steel spoon
Wooden spoon
Metal spatula
Rubber scraper
Juicer
Sieve
Zester (optional)
4 sheets of 12-inch-square kitchen parchment or foil

START-TO-FINISH STEPS

Thirty minutes ahead: For snapper recipe, soften *achiote* seeds: In small saucepan, bring 1 cup water to a boil. Add *achiote* seeds and remove pan from heat. Let soak until ready to use.

1. Prepare vegetables, herbs, and jalapeño and serrano peppers for seviche, red snapper, and rice recipes. Be sure to wear rubber gloves when handling hot peppers and to use the tip of a knife for seeding the jalapeños.
2. With zester or paring knife, peel citrus fruit for snapper recipe, being careful to avoid the white pith. Juice fruit for snapper recipe and juice lime for seviche recipe.
3. Follow seviche recipe steps 1 and 2.
4. Follow rice recipe steps 1 and 2. While rice is coming to a boil, rinse processor or blender jar, then follow step 3.
5. While rice is cooking, follow snapper recipe steps 1 through 4 and seviche recipe step 3.
6. Follow snapper recipe steps 5 and 6, and serve seviche.
7. Follow snapper recipe step 7 and rice recipe step 4.

RECIPES

Oyster Seviche

24 extra-small shucked oysters with liquor
½ cup diced red bell peppper
⅓ cup chopped fresh coriander
1 tablespoon minced shallots
2 tablespoons virgin olive oil
½ cup diced California green chilies, approximately
1 fresh or canned jalapeño pepper, seeded and minced
1 fresh or canned serrano pepper, including seeds, minced
¼ cup fresh lime juice

1. Remove all bits of shell from oysters and strain liquor.
2. In large stainless steel bowl, combine red pepper, chopped coriander, shallots, and oil. Add chilies to taste and reserve remaining chilies. Add oysters, liquor, and lime juice to marinade and stir to combine. Cover and refrigerate until ready to serve.

3. Just before serving, taste again and add more chilies, if desired. Divide among individual bowls.

Baked Red Snapper with Chili Sauce

Peel of 2 oranges, approximately ¼ cup
Peel of 1 lime, approximately 2 teaspoons
Peel of 1 lemon, approximately 1 tablespoon
1½ cups fresh orange juice
2 tablespoons fresh lemon juice
3 tablespoons fresh lime juice
⅓ cup virgin olive oil
1 tablespoon rice wine vinegar
1 large clove garlic, peeled
4 tablespoons ancho chili powder
3 tablespoons New Mexico chili powder
3 tablespoons California chili powder
2 teaspoons salt
1 teaspoon dried *achiote* seeds, softened
½ teaspoon freshly ground black pepper
Dash of Cayenne pepper
Four ¾-inch-thick fillets of red snapper or any white, meaty fish such as tilefish, grouper, halibut, or scrod (each about 8 ounces)

1. Preheat oven to 450 degrees.
2. For sauce, grind citrus peels in food processor or blender. Gradually add all ingredients except fish and process 1 minute, or until smooth.
3. Wipe fillets with damp paper towels.
4. Place each fillet on 12-inch-square sheet of kitchen parchment or round of aluminum foil. Spoon 2 tablespoons sauce over each fillet and scrape remaining sauce into small saucepan. Tightly fold edges of parchment or foil.
5. Place fish packets in baking dish and bake 8 minutes.
6. Meanwhile, bring remaining sauce to a simmer over medium-high heat, stirring frequently. Reduce heat to low and cook sauce, uncovered, until fish is ready.
7. Remove fish from oven and open packets. With metal spatula, transfer fish to dinner plates and top with sauce.

Green Rice

2 large leaves Romaine lettuce, coarsely chopped
1 cup fresh coriander leaves
1 fresh jalapeño pepper, seeded and minced
1 large clove garlic
1 cup long-grain white rice
1 tablespoon unsalted butter
1 teaspoon salt

1. In food processor or blender, blend lettuce, coriander, jalapeño pepper, garlic, and 2 cups water until smooth.
2. Scrape mixture into medium-size saucepan. Add rice, butter, and salt, and stir to combine. Bring to a boil over high heat, stir once, and cover tightly.
3. Reduce heat to medium-low and simmer 15 minutes, or until all liquid is absorbed.
4. Toss rice with fork and serve alongside snapper.

Salmon à la Tartare
Poached Oysters with Saffron-Cream Sauce

Serve the salmon appetizer garnished with lemon slices and mint sprigs, followed by pasta with an oyster-spinach sauce.

Like raw beef, raw fish has its aficionados in many countries. For the best tasting dish, the fish must be as fresh as possible.

Oysters need only gentle poaching to cook through. If boiled, the oysters will shrink and toughen. Saffron is the world's costliest spice, but a little of it goes a long way.

WHAT TO DRINK

Salmon and oysters are straightforward in flavor but rich. The ideal accompaniment is a Chardonnay-based wine: either a California Chardonnay or a white Burgundy.

SHOPPING LIST AND STAPLES

20 freshly shucked oysters with liquor
8-ounce fillet of salmon
Medium-size red bell pepper
6 ounces young spinach, preferably small-leaf
½ pound onions
2 shallots
1 bunch chives
Small bunch parsley
1 lemon
½ pint heavy cream

6 tablespoons unsalted butter
2 cups fish stock preferably homemade (see page 13), or 8-ounce bottle clam juice
¼ cup olive oil
1 tablespoon unsalted mayonnaise, preferably homemade
12 ounces fresh spinach linguine or fettuccine
1 baguette
1 to 1½ teaspoons saffron threads, lightly packed
Salt and freshly ground white pepper

UTENSILS

Food processor (optional)
Large stockpot
Large sauté pan
Small saucepan
13 x 9 x 2-inch baking pan
Plate
Large stainless steel or glass bowl plus additional slightly larger bowl or saucepan
Salad spinner (optional)
Colander
Measuring cups and spoons
Chef's knife
Bread knife
Wooden spoon
Slotted spoon
Tongs
Pastry brush
Fine-mesh sieve

START-TO-FINISH STEPS

1. Follow oyster recipe steps 1 through 4.
2. Prepare vegetables and herbs, and squeeze enough lemon to measure 1 teaspoon juice.
3. Follow salmon recipe step 1 and oyster recipe step 5.
4. While saffron liquid is reducing, follow salmon recipe steps 2 through 4. Remove bread from oven.
5. Follow oyster recipe steps 6 through 8.
6. While sauce is reducing, follow salmon recipe step 5 and serve.
7. Follow oyster recipe steps 9 through 11 and serve.

RECIPES

Salmon à la Tartare

1 baguette
2 tablespoons unsalted butter
8-ounce fillet of salmon, chilled
2 tablespoons chopped chives
2 tablespoons chopped parsley
2 tablespoons minced shallots
¼ cup olive oil
1 tablespoon unsalted mayonaise, preferably homemade
1 teaspoon lemon juice
Pinch of salt
Pinch of freshly ground white pepper

1. Preheat oven to 350 degrees.
2. To make croutons: With bread knife, cut baguette into ⅓-inch slices. In small saucepan, melt butter over medium heat. In baking pan, arrange slices in a single layer and brush one side of each with melted butter. Toast in oven until lightly browned, 10 to 15 minutes.
3. While bread is toasting, wipe salmon with damp paper towels. Using food processor fitted with steel blade or chef's knife, mince salmon. Do not overprocess.
4. In large stainless steel or glass bowl resting in slightly larger bowl of ice, combine salmon, chives, parsley, shallots, oil, mayonnaise, lemon juice, salt, and pepper and toss to combine. Cover bowl and refrigerate.
5. Spoon an equal amount of salmon tartare onto each crouton and divide croutons among 4 plates.

Poached Oysters with Saffron-Cream Sauce

Salt
6 ounces young spinach leaves, preferably small-leaf
20 freshly shucked oysters with liquor
2 cups fish stock, or 1 cup clam juice mixed with 1 cup water
1 to 1½ teaspoons saffron threads, lightly packed
1⅔ cups diced onions
½ cup diced red bell pepper
1 cup heavy cream
4 tablespoons unsalted butter
12 ounces fresh spinach linguine or fettuccine
Freshly ground pepper

1. In large stockpot, bring 2 quarts water plus 2 teaspoons salt to a boil over high heat.
2. Wash spinach thoroughly and remove stems.
3. Blanch spinach 1 minute. With slotted spoon, transfer spinach to colander and refresh immediately under cold running water. Cover pot and reserve cooking water.
4. Remove all bits of shell from oysters. Strain liquor through fine sieve into measuring cup. In large sauté pan, combine liquor and enough stock to make 2 cups and bring to a simmer. Remove pan from heat, add saffron, onion, and red pepper, and swirl. Set aside.
5. Bring saffron liquid to a boil over medium-high heat and reduce liquid to about 1 cup, 10 to 15 minutes.
6. Lower heat to a simmer, add oysters, and cook 2 minutes, or just until edges begin to curl. With slotted spoon, quickly transfer oysters to plate to avoid overcooking.
7. Add enough fresh water to reserved cooking water to measure 4 quarts. Cover and bring to a boil over high heat.
8. For sauce, add cream and butter to saffron liquid and reduce liquid by one third, about 15 minutes.
9. Add pasta to boiling salted water and cook 2 to 3 minutes from time water returns to a boil.
10. While pasta is cooking, return oysters to sauce to reheat. Stir in spinach and add salt and pepper to taste.
11. Drain pasta in colander. Push sauce solids to one side of sauté pan, leaving sauce behind. Add pasta to sauce and, with tongs, turn pasta until evenly coated. Divide pasta among 4 plates and top with oyster mixture.

Elisabeth Thorstensson

MENU 1 (Right)
Fillets of Sole in Herb Butter
Riced Potatoes with Parsley
Sautéed Snow Peas with Water Chestnuts

MENU 2
Seafood Curry Chowder
Bibb Lettuce, Avocado, and Tomato Salad

MENU 3
Chicken Liver Mousse
Fillets of Brook Trout with Mushroom Sauce
Spicy Rice

S wedish cooking, like that of Scandinavia in general, is straightforward and down to earth. Swedish cooks use fresh produce, dairy products, subtle seasonings, and most important, just-caught fish. Elisabeth Thorstensson grew up at lakeside and often caught the family's fish for dinner. Very early, she learned how to prepare fish for poaching, pan frying, and baking, all techniques her family commonly uses and that she employs in her menus here.

She frequently returns to Sweden to gather cooking suggestions. In addition, she has also incorporated a variety of new ideas into these three menus. Menu 1 consists of three dishes: fillets of sole in herb butter, riced potatoes, and a vegetable dish of sautéed snow peas with water chestnuts. The presentation of the meal is designed for visual effect—the green herb butter contrasts with the white fish and sauce, and there is a similar color contrast in the vegetable dishes.

Elisabeth Thorstensson first tasted a version of Menu 2's curry chowder at her sister's house in Sweden. Here, the chef has varied her sister's recipe by adding chunks of fresh fish.

In Menu 3, she presents a chicken liver mousse flavored with Cognac, brandy, or sherry, and sautéed fillets of brook trout served with mushroom sauce. The rice is seasoned with turmeric, a spice often used in Indian and Asian recipes, which turns the rice a golden color.

Serve this dinner on individual plates for a pleasing appearance. The fillets of sole are topped with browned bread-crumbs and surrounded by a wine sauce, the riced potatoes are studded with parsley and chopped pimiento and the snow peas are garnished with sliced water chestnuts.

Fillets of Sole in Herb Butter
Riced Potatoes with Parsley
Sautéed Snow Peas with Water Chestnuts

Fillets of sole are ideal for rolling up, then baking, as in this recipe. The accompanying wine sauce is made with scallions, parsley, and tarragon. You can substitute either fresh flounder or frozen flounder.

Chinese water chestnuts are not nuts at all but tubers of an aquatic plant. They come in cans in the Oriental foods section of most supermarkets. Because they retain their crispness after cooking, they are particularly good sautéed with fresh snow peas.

WHAT TO DRINK

Buy a good white Graves or a crisp California Sauvignon Blanc and use the same wine to make the sauce for the sole.

SHOPPING LIST AND STAPLES

4 skinless fillets of sole, flounder, or scrod (each about 8 ounces)
2 large baking potatoes, preferably Idaho (about 1¼ pounds total weight)
¾ pound snow peas
Small bunch scallions
Small bunch fresh parsley
Small bunch fresh tarragon, or ½ teaspoon dried
1 lemon
1 egg
½ pint heavy cream
4 tablespoons unsalted butter
8-ounce jar pimientos
8-ounce can water chestnuts
3 tablespoons vegetable oil
1 slice day-old white bread
Salt and freshly ground pepper
1 cup dry white wine, preferably same as dinner wine

UTENSILS

Food processor or blender
Large heavy-gauge skillet
2 medium-size saucepans, one with cover
13 x 9-inch baking dish
8 x 8-inch baking pan
2 medium-size bowls
Small bowl
Colander
Measuring cups and spoons
Paring knife
Chef's knife
Wooden spatula
Rubber spatula
Ricer or potato masher
Coarse sieve
Vegetable peeler

START-TO-FINISH STEPS

1. Prepare scallions and tarragon for sole recipe and parsley for sole and potatoes recipes. Chop pimiento for potatoes recipe.
2. Follow sole recipe steps 1 through 6.
3. Follow potato recipe step 1.
4. While potatoes are coming to a boil, follow sole recipe steps 7 and 8. Then follow potatoes recipe step 2.
5. While sole and potatoes are cooking, follow snow peas recipe steps 1 and 2.
6. Five minutes before sole and potatoes are done, follow snow peas recipe step 3.
7. Follow potatoes recipe step 3, sole recipe step 9, and serve with snow peas.

RECIPES

Fillets of Sole in Herb Butter

4 skinless fillets of sole, flounder, or scrod (each about 8 ounces)
1 lemon
1 egg
4 tablespoons unsalted butter
1 tablespoon chopped scallion
1 tablespoon chopped fresh parsley
1½ teaspoons chopped fresh tarragon, or ½ teaspoon dried
1 cup heavy cream
1 cup dry white wine (preferably same as dinner wine)
Salt
Freshly ground pepper
1 slice day-old white bread

1. Wipe fillets with damp paper towels.
2. In 13 x 9-inch baking dish, arrange fillets in single layer. Squeeze lemon juice over them and let stand.

3. Separate egg, dropping yolk into food processor or blender. Reserve white for another use. Combine butter with egg yolk and process until smooth. Add scallion, parsley, and tarragon, and blend well. With rubber spatula, scrape mixture into small bowl and set aside.

4. In medium-size saucepan, reduce cream by half over medium-high heat, about 10 to 15 minutes. Add wine and boil 1 minute. Season with salt and pepper to taste. Set aside.

5. Cut crust off bread and rub bread through coarse sieve onto piece of aluminum foil or wax paper.

6. Preheat oven to 450 degrees.

7. Fold each fillet in three, as if you were folding a letter, and place flat side down in 8 x 8-inch baking pan. Spread herb butter evenly over fillets and sprinkle with bread crumbs. Pour cream-wine mixture carefully into dish without touching top of fish, being careful not to disturb bread crumbs.

8. Bake until bread crumbs are golden-brown and fish is firm, 15 to 20 minutes.

9. Remove fish from oven. Using spatula, transfer fillets to dinner plates.

Riced Potatoes with Parsley

2 large baking potatoes, preferably Idaho (about
   1¼ pounds total weight)
Salt and freshly ground pepper
2 tablespoons minced fresh parsley
1 tablespoon chopped pimiento

1. Peel potatoes and cut in thirds. In medium-size saucepan, cover potatoes with 2 inches of cold water. Cover pan and bring to a boil over high heat.

2. Reduce heat to moderate and boil potatoes just until tender, 15 to 20 minutes. Drain thoroughly in colander and, off heat, return to saucepan to dry, 1 to 2 minutes.

3. With ricer, rice potatoes directly into medium-size bowl. Or, using potato masher, mash potatoes. Season with salt and pepper to taste, and sprinkle with parsley and pimiento. Divide among individual dinner plates.

Sautéed Snow Peas with Water Chestnuts

¾ pound snow peas
1 cup drained water chestnuts
3 tablespoons vegetable oil
Salt and freshly ground pepper

1. Snap off ends of snow peas and remove strings. In medium-size bowl, cover snow peas with cold water.

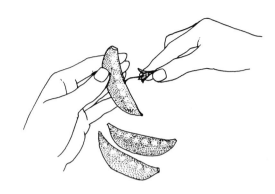

2. With chef's knife, cut water chestnuts into ¼-inch-thick slices. Pat dry with paper towels and set aside.

3. In colander, drain snow peas and pat dry with paper towels. In large heavy-gauge skillet, heat oil until hot but not smoking. Add snow peas and sauté, stirring with wooden spatula, about 2 minutes. Add water chestnuts and sauté mixture just until snow peas are crisp-tender, another 2 minutes. Season with salt and pepper to taste.

ADDED TOUCH

Gazpacho, the famous "liquid salad" of Spanish cuisine, requires a few minutes of peeling and chopping to ready the vegetables for the blender or food processor. Be careful not to overprocess the vegetables—the soup should have a crunchy texture.

Gazpacho

½ cup chopped scallions
½ cup chopped fresh tomato
½ cup chopped red bell pepper
½ cup chopped green bell pepper
½ cup chopped cucumber
Sprigs of parsley (optional)
16-ounce can whole peeled Italian plum tomatoes
2 tablespoons vegetable oil
2 tablespoons cider vinegar
Large clove garlic
1 teaspoon salt
1 teaspoon freshly ground pepper

1. Prepare fresh vegetables. If using parsley for garnish, separate sprigs, wash, and pat dry.

2. In food processor or blender, combine undrained canned tomatoes, oil, vinegar, garlic, salt, and pepper, and blend until smooth. Pour into large serving bowl.

3. In food processor or blender, combine scallions, fresh tomato, red and green bell peppers, and cucumber. Pulse or blend until vegetables are chopped but not mushy. With wooden spoon, stir chopped vegetables into tomato mixture and taste for seasoning. Cover bowl with plastic wrap and refrigerate until chilled, about 1 hour.

4. Divide soup among individual bowls and garnish each serving with parsley sprigs if desired.

Seafood Curry Chowder
Bibb Lettuce, Avocado, and Tomato Salad

For this informal meal, ladle the chowder into soup bowls set on dinner plates and serve the salad on the side.

Elisabeth Thorstensson combines two delicate lean fish with shrimp for this main-course chowder. Curry is a combination of several spices. A commercially blended curry powder, from the supermarket, which is suitable for this recipe, contains some combination of these spices: chili, turmeric, ginger, coriander, cumin, cloves, cinnamon, fenugreek, and black pepper.

WHAT TO DRINK

A dry Riesling from California, Alsace, or Germany would suit this menu.

SHOPPING LIST AND STAPLES

½ pound medium-size shrimp (10 to 12), shelled and deveined
1 fillet of flounder (about 11 ounces)
1 fillet of halibut, scrod, or cod (about 8 ounces)
4 tomatoes, preferably Italian plum (about 1 pound total weight)
2 heads Bibb lettuce
1 avocado
Small yellow onion
Medium-size clove garlic

Small bunch dill
2 lemons
½ pint heavy cream
4 tablespoons unsalted butter
10-ounce package frozen tiny peas
2 cups chicken stock, preferably homemade (see page 13),
    or canned
2 cups fish stock, preferably homemade (see page 13),
    or two 8-ounce bottles clam juice
¾ cup vegetable oil
¼ cup red wine vinegar
1 teaspoon Dijon mustard
1 teaspoon chili sauce
¼ cup flour
1 teaspoon curry powder (approximately)
Salt
Freshly ground pepper

UTENSILS

Food processor or blender
Large heavy-gauge saucepan with cover
Medium-size bowl
Plate
Salad spinner (optional)
Measuring cups and spoons
Chef's knife
Paring knife
Wooden spoon
Ladle
Whisk
Juicer
Medium-size jar with lid

START-TO-FINISH STEPS

1. For chowder recipe, transfer frozen peas from package to plate to defrost.
2. Juice lemon for chowder recipe and salad recipe.
3. Follow salad recipe steps 1 and 2.
4. Follow chowder recipe steps 1 and 2.
5. While stock simmers, follow salad recipe steps 3 through 5.
6. Follow chowder recipe step 3 and salad recipe step 6.
7. Follow chowder recipe steps 4 and 5, and serve with salad.

RECIPES

Seafood Curry Chowder

1 fillet of flounder (about 11 ounces)
1 fillet of halibut, scrod, or cod (about 8 ounces)
½ pound medium-size shrimp (10 to 12), shelled and
    deveined
2 tablespoons lemon juice
4 tablespoons unsalted butter
¼ cup flour
1 teaspoon curry powder, approximately

2 cups fish stock or clam juice
2 cups chicken stock
2 teaspoons salt
1 teaspoon freshly ground pepper
½ cup frozen tiny peas, thawed
½ cup heavy cream
2 tablespoons finely chopped dill

1. Wipe fish fillets with damp paper towels. With chef's knife, cut halibut into ½-inch pieces. Cut flounder into ¾-inch pieces. Cut shrimps in half lengthwise. Transfer fish and shrimps to medium-size bowl, sprinkle with lemon juice, and toss to combine. Set aside.
2. In large heavy-gauge saucepan, melt butter over medium-low heat. Add flour and curry powder to taste, and whisk until thoroughly blended. Cook, stirring with whisk, 3 minutes. Whisking constantly, slowly add fish stock and chicken stock. Add salt and pepper and, stirring occasionally, bring to a boil over medium-high heat. Reduce heat, cover, and simmer 10 minutes.
3. Add fish pieces, shrimps, peas, and cream, and stir to combine. Simmer 1 minute.
4. Remove pan from heat and whisk in dill.
5. Ladle chowder into individual soup bowls set on dinner plates.

Bibb Lettuce, Avocado, and Tomato Salad

Medium-size clove garlic
Small yellow onion
1 teaspoon chili sauce
1 teaspoon Dijon mustard
¼ cup red wine vinegar
¾ cup vegetable oil
½ teaspoon salt
½ teaspoon pepper
2 heads Bibb lettuce
4 tomatoes, preferably Italian plum (about 1 pound total
    weight)
1 avocado
2 tablespoons lemon juice
1 teaspoon finely chopped dill

1. Peel garlic and onion. Cut onion into quarters.
2. In medium-size jar, combine garlic, onion, chili sauce, mustard, vinegar, ¼ cup water, vegetable oil, salt, and pepper. Shake well to mix dressing and refrigerate until ready to serve.
3. Wash lettuce and dry in salad spinner or pat dry with paper towels. Wash tomatoes and cut crosswise into ¼-inch-thick slices. Set aside.
4. On individual dinner plates, arrange lettuce, leaving room for soup bowls.
5. Peel avocado and halve lengthwise. Twist to separate halves. Remove pit and discard. Cut each half lengthwise into 6 slices. Divide avocado and tomato slices among individual plates and arrange on lettuce. Sprinkle lemon juice over avocado slices.
6. Shake dressing to recombine and spoon over tomatoes and avocado. Sprinkle each serving with dill.

Chicken Liver Mousse
Fillets of Brook Trout with Mushroom Sauce
Spicy Rice

Serve the chicken liver mousse appetizer in small crocks with sliced pumpernickel bread. A garnish of lime slices and strips of red pepper provide a striking color contrast to the fillets of brook trout with mushroom sauce.

Fillets of brook trout are the entrée for this simple family meal. For the mousse appetizer, buy plump odorless chicken livers. To avoid any bitter taste, the cook recommends not cutting into the livers before sautéing them.

WHAT TO DRINK

Any dry white wine goes with trout; try a California Sauvignon Blanc or an Italian Pinot Bianco.

SHOPPING LIST AND STAPLES

1 pound chicken livers
8 fillets of brook trout, rainbow trout, or perch (1½ to
    2 pounds total weight)
1 pound small white mushrooms
Medium-size yellow onion
3 shallots
2 cloves garlic
Small bunch fresh parsley
Small bunch fresh thyme, or pinch of dried
2 lemons
½ pint heavy cream
2 sticks plus 2 tablespoons unsalted butter
2 cups chicken stock, preferably homemade (see page 13)
    or canned
2 tablespoons vegetable oil
1 cup long-grain white rice
1 cup flour
Small loaf pumpernickel bread
2 tablespoons pine nuts
1 teaspoon turmeric
1 teaspoon ground coriander
Salt and freshly ground pepper
1 cup dry white wine
2 tablespoons Cognac, brandy, or dry sherry

UTENSILS

Food processor or blender
Large heavy-gauge skillet
Small heavy-gauge skillet
2 medium-size saucepans, one with cover
13 x 9 x 2-inch baking pan
Medium-size bowl
Measuring cups and spoons
Chef's knife

Paring knife
2 wooden spoons
Wooden spatula
Rubber spatula
Slotted spatula
Juicer

START-TO-FINISH STEPS

1. Follow mousse recipe steps 1 through 3.
2. Follow mushroom sauce recipe steps 1 through 4.
3. Follow mousse recipe steps 4 and 5.
4. Follow rice recipe steps 1 and 2.
5. Follow trout recipe steps 1 through 3.
6. Follow rice recipe step 3.
7. Follow mousse recipe step 6 and serve.
8. Follow trout recipe steps 4 and 5, mushroom sauce recipe step 5, rice recipe step 4, and serve.

RECIPES

Chicken Liver Mousse

1 pound chicken livers
1 stick plus 3 tablespoons unsalted butter
2 tablespoons chopped shallots
½ teaspoon salt
½ teaspoon freshly ground pepper
2 tablespoons Cognac, brandy, or dry sherry
4 thin slices pumpernickel bread, halved

1. Remove membrane and fat from chicken livers, rinse under cold water, and gently pat dry with paper towels.
2. In large heavy-gauge skillet, heat 3 tablespoons butter over medium-high heat until slightly brown. Add livers and sauté 2 to 3 minutes. Add shallots, salt, and pepper, and cook, stirring, 2 minutes.
3. Transfer livers, shallots, and pan juices to bowl of food processor or blender and process until smooth. Add Cognac, brandy, or sherry and process briefly. Turn mixture into medium-size bowl and set aside to cool. Rinse skillet and dry.
4. In food processor or blender, cream remaining butter.
5. Add creamed butter to cooled liver mixture and stir until blended. Chill in freezer 15 minutes.
6. Remove mousse from freezer and divide among individual ramekins.

Fillets of Brook Trout

2 lemons
8 fillets of brook trout, rainbow trout, or perch
1 cup flour
2 teaspoons salt
1 teaspoon freshly ground pepper
1 teaspoon fresh thyme, or pinch of dried
4 tablespoons unsalted butter
Mushroom sauce (see following recipe)

1. Preheat oven to 200 degrees.
2. Juice 2 lemons and strain out pits. Wipe fish fillets with damp paper towels and arrange in single layer in baking pan. Pour lemon juice over fish. Set aside.
3. On sheet of foil, combine flour, salt, pepper, and thyme.
4. In large heavy-gauge skillet used for livers, heat 2 tablespoons butter over medium heat until lightly browned. While butter is browning, dredge 4 fillets in flour mixture. Fry fillets until golden brown, about 2 minutes on each side. Using slotted spatula, remove from pan and drain on paper towels. Transfer fillets to 2 dinner plates and keep warm in oven. Repeat process for remaining fillets.
5. When ready to serve, remove plates from oven and spoon sauce over fish.

Mushroom Sauce

1 pound small white mushrooms
1 clove garlic
3 tablespoons unsalted butter
1 cup dry white wine
1 cup heavy cream
Salt and freshly ground pepper

1. Wipe mushrooms clean with damp paper towels. Trim off stems and cut lengthwise into thin slices.
2. Peel garlic and crush with flat side of chef's knife.
3. In medium-size saucepan, melt butter over medium heat. Add garlic and sauté, stirring, 1 minute. Remove garlic and discard. Add mushrooms and cook, stirring, until liquid has almost evaporated, about 10 minutes.
4. Raise heat to medium-high. Add wine and cook, stirring occasionally, until reduced by half, about 5 minutes. Remove pan from heat and set aside.
5. Add heavy cream and cook, stirring, over medium heat until sauce has thickened slightly, 3 to 4 minutes. Do not boil. Season with salt and freshly ground pepper to taste. Keep warm over very low heat until ready to use.

Spicy Rice

2 tablespoons pine nuts
2 tablespoons vegetable oil
1 clove garlic, minced
Medium-size yellow onion, minced
1 cup long-grain white rice
2 cups chicken stock
1 teaspoon turmeric
1 teaspoon ground coriander
Salt and freshly ground pepper
1 tablespoon finely chopped parsley

1. In small heavy-gauge skillet, toast pine nuts over medium-high heat about 2 minutes, shaking skillet from time to time to keep pine nuts from scorching.
2. In medium-size saucepan, heat oil over medium-high heat. Add garlic and onion, and sauté, stirring frequently, until translucent, 3 to 4 minutes. Lower heat to medium, add rice, and cook, stirring, another 2 minutes.
3. Add stock, pine nuts, turmeric, and coriander, and stir until blended. Bring to a boil over high heat. Reduce heat to low, cover, and simmer 18 minutes.
4. Add salt and pepper to taste. With fork, fluff rice.

Linda Johnson

MENU 1 (Left)
Prawns with Green Peppercorns
Snow Peas and Jícama
Orzo with Poppy Seeds

MENU 2
Steamed Mussels
Brown Rice with Roasted Red Pepper
Asparagus Vinaigrette with Pecans

MENU 3
Bourbon-Basted Salmon
Bulgur Pilaf
Spinach and Kiwi Salad

L inda Johnson, who has a Master's Degree in Foods and Nutrition from San Francisco State University, says, "I believe that it is easy to eat nutritiously yet have interesting and delicious foods." Although she uses little salt, she does use alternate flavor enhancers, such as lemons, limes, herbs, spices, and a variety of vegetables.

She serves fish and shellfish, low-fat protein sources, with sauces that contain a minimum of fat or oil. The prawns of Menu 1 are quickly sautéed with shallots and green peppercorns, and then flambéed with Cognac. The mussels of Menu 2 are steamed in a flavorful variety of ingredients, including tarragon, garlic, artichoke hearts, and white wine. The salmon fillets of Menu 3 are brushed with a bourbon, soy sauce, and olive oil baste.

Linda Johnson's menus incorporate various unrefined grains, nuts, seeds, and vegetables that provide fiber and complex carbohydrates. For instance, in Menu 1 snow peas are combined with jícama, a crunchy Mexican vegetable, for a lightly seasoned accompaniment to the prawns. In Menu 2, brown rice and asparagus spears with pecans are the fiber sources. Menu 3 features bulgur (cracked wheat) and spinach.

For this meal, prawns with green peppercorns are flambéed with Cognac, then arranged on dinner plates, accompanied by stir-fried snow peas with julienned jícama and orzo with poppy seeds. If you wish, offer your guests chopsticks for eating this dinner.

Prawns with Green Peppercorns
Snow Peas and Jícama
Orzo with Poppy Seeds

Jumbo shrimp, often called "prawns" in American markets, are cooked when they firm up and turn an orange-white color. They are seasoned with green peppercorns—fresh unripened pepper berries—which add piquancy but not excessive spiciness. Green peppercorns are available packed in either water or vinegar. They are perishable, so refrigerate them after opening. Vinegar-packed peppercorns will last 1 month; water-packed will last 1 week.

Jícama, a bulbous brown root, has juicy white flesh similar to that of water chestnuts. Jícama is sold either whole or cut into pieces, which are wrapped in plastic. Choose firm, well-shaped whole roots with no bruises or other signs of age. Smaller jícama are less likely to be woody than are large ones. Store whole jícama in a plastic bag in the refrigerator. Keep cut pieces covered with water, refrigerated. If jícama is unavailable, use kohlrabi, an acceptable substitute that has a mild turnip-like flavor.

Orzo is a rice-shaped pasta popular in Greek cooking. It is usually served in soups or as an accompaniment to lamb. Here, the cook seasons the orzo with poppy seeds, which are available in the spice section of most supermarkets.

WHAT TO DRINK

If you want a soft wine, choose a Soave or a Lugana; if you want a wine to interact with the dishes, try a good dry German Riesling from a named village.

SHOPPING LIST AND STAPLES

1½ pounds jumbo shrimps or prawns
¾ pound snow peas
¼ pound jícama or kohlrabi
3 large shallots
Medium-size lime
7 tablespoons unsalted butter
¼ pound Parmesan cheese
1 tablespoon virgin olive oil
2-ounce can green peppercorns
8-ounce package orzo or other small pasta
1½-ounce can poppy seeds
Salt and freshly ground pepper
¼ cup Cognac or brandy

UTENSILS

Wok (optional)

Medium-size skillet plus one additional (if not using wok)
Medium-size saucepan with cover
Small saucepan with cover
2 medium-size bowls, one heatproof
Colander
Sieve
Measuring cups and spoons
Chef's knife
Paring knife
Wooden spoon
Wooden spatula
Grater
Juicer (optional)

START-TO-FINISH STEPS

1. Chop shallots for prawns recipe, grate cheese for pasta recipe, and juice lime for snow peas recipe.
2. Follow prawns recipe step 1.
3. Follow snow peas recipe steps 1 through 3.
4. Follow orzo recipe steps 1 and 2, and prawns recipe step 2.
5. Follow orzo recipe step 3.
6. While orzo is cooking, follow snow peas recipe step 4 and prawns recipe step 3.
7. While shallots are cooking, follow orzo recipe steps 4 and 5.
8. Follow prawns recipe steps 4 through 6, snow peas recipe step 5, and serve with orzo.

RECIPES

Prawns with Green Peppercorns

1½ pounds shrimps or prawns
1 teaspoon green peppercorns
3 tablespoons unsalted butter
5 tablespoons chopped shallots
Salt
Freshly ground pepper
¼ cup Cognac

1. Shell and devein prawns (see page 11). Place in colander, rinse under cold running water, drain, and pat dry with paper towels. Transfer to medium-size bowl, cover with plastic wrap, and refrigerate.
2. If using vinegar-packed peppercorns, place in sieve and rinse under cold running water. Drain and pat dry. If using water-packed, drain and pat dry. Set aside.

3. In medium-size skillet, melt butter over medium heat. Add shallots and peppercorns, and sauté until shallots are transparent, 2 to 3 minutes. Place dinner plates in oven to warm.

4. Raise heat to high, add prawns, and sauté, turning with wooden spatula, until flesh turn pink, 3 to 4 minutes. Season with salt and pepper to taste.

5. Pour Cognac over prawns and turn off heat. Standing away from stove, avert your face and ignite Cognac by carefully holding lit match at lip of skillet. Shake skillet gently until flame dies out.

6. Divide prawns among warm dinner plates and top with pan juices.

Snow Peas and Jícama

¾ pound snow peas
¼ pound jícama or kohlrabi
1 tablespoon virgin olive oil
Salt
Freshly ground pepper
Juice of 1 lime

1. Preheat oven to 200 degrees.
2. In colander, rinse snow peas under cold running water and drain. Pat dry with paper towels. Snap off ends and remove strings.
3. Peel jícama or kohlrabi, rinse under cold water, and pat dry with paper towels. Slice into ¼-inch julienne strips.
4. In wok or medium-size skillet, heat oil over high heat. When drop of water evaporates on contact, add snow peas and jícama or kohlrabi. Cook about 6 minutes, stirring constantly with wooden spatula, until vegetables are crisp-tender. Add salt and pepper to taste. Turn into heatproof bowl, cover with foil, and keep warm in oven until ready to serve.
5. Just before serving, pour lime juice over vegetables and toss. Divide among individual plates.

Orzo with Poppy Seeds

Salt
1 cup orzo or other small pasta
4 tablespoons unsalted butter
1½ tablespoons poppy seeds
1 cup grated Parmesan cheese

1. In medium-size saucepan, bring 1½ quarts water and 1½ teaspoons salt to a boil over medium-high heat.

2. While water is coming to a boil, melt butter in small saucepan over medium heat and stir in poppy seeds. Partially cover pan and turn off heat, but leave on burner.
3. Add pasta to boiling water and stir. Return to a boil and stir again, cover pot, and cook over medium heat until pasta is *al dente*, 7 to 10 minutes.
4. When pasta is cooked, remove pan from heat and add 1 cup cold water.
5. Turn pasta into colander or sieve, shake to remove excess water, and return pasta to pan. With wooden spoon, stir butter and poppy seed mixture to recombine. Add to pasta and stir. Add cheese and toss to combine. Season with salt to taste. Cover saucepan to keep warm until ready to serve.

LEFTOVER SUGGESTION

Cut leftover jícama into sticks for use as an hors d'oeuvre and serve with a dip. Jícama is also an excellent addition to green salads and is a perfect substitute for water chestnuts in Chinese stir-fry dishes.

ADDED TOUCH

This dessert will be lower in fat if you use partly skimmed-milk farmer cheese. You can spread the cheese, enriched with currants and almonds, on the crackers or on the fruit slices.

Sweet Cheese with Crackers and Assorted Fruit

1 cup farmer cheese or baker's or hoop cheese
¼ teaspoon vanilla extract
2 tablespoons currants
2 tablespoons chopped almonds
Assortment of cold fruit (apples, pears, melon, peaches, kiwi, or other fruit in season)
Water biscuits

1. At least 2 hours before serving, place cheese in medium-size bowl and stir with rubber spatula until spreadable. Add vanilla and stir until blended. Add currants and almonds, and stir until evenly distributed.
2. Turn mixture into crock or serving bowl, cover, and refrigerate.
3. Just before serving, slice fruit and arrange on platter around crock of cheese. Serve with water biscuits.

Steamed Mussels
Brown Rice with Roasted Red Pepper
Asparagus Vinaigrette with Pecans

Mussels, which are low in fat, are generally available nationwide all year long. However, depending on their source, they are at their peak during different seasons. For this recipe, buy small mussels, which are more tender than the larger ones, for uniform cooking. The mussels are steamed in a liquid containing herbs, seasonings, and either artichoke hearts or bottoms. These terms are often used interchangeably, but the heart is a portion of the bottom with several of the tender inner leaves. The bottom is only the circular fleshy base of the artichoke.

A platter of mussels and artichoke hearts accompanied by asparagus spears and brown rice make a perfect informal dinner. For convenience, you may wish to provide each guest with an extra bowl for empty shells.

To simplify preparation of the asparagus dish, buy shelled pecans and refrigerate leftovers in an air-tight container.

WHAT TO DRINK

Artichokes, asparagus, and vinaigrette dressing do not go well with wine, except perhaps a simple dry white, such as French Muscadet or Italian Verdicchio.

SHOPPING LIST AND STAPLES

3 pounds mussels
1 pound asparagus
Medium-size red bell pepper

6 cloves garlic
1 bunch scallions
Medium-size bunch fresh parsley
1 bunch fresh chives, or 2 tablespoons frozen
Small bunch fresh tarragon, or ½ teaspoon dried
5 tablespoons unsalted butter
9-ounce package frozen artichoke hearts or bottoms
¼ cup plus 2 tablespoons virgin olive oil
2 tablespoons red wine vinegar
1 cup brown rice
6¼-ounce bag shelled pecans
Dash of dry mustard
Pinch of sugar
Salt and freshly ground pepper
¾ cup dry white wine

UTENSILS

Medium-size skillet with cover
Large saucepan with cover
Medium-size saucepan with tight-fitting cover
Plate
Large bowl
Small bowl
Colander
Measuring cups and spoons
Chef's knife
Paring knife
Long 2-pronged fork
Stiff scrubbing brush
Small brown paper bag

START-TO-FINISH STEPS

1. Defrost artichoke hearts for mussels recipe: Place in colander and set under cold running water. Drain and chop enough to measure 1 cup.

2. Follow brown rice recipe steps 1 and 2.

3. Follow mussels recipe step 1.

4. Follow asparagus recipe steps 1 through 4.

5. Follow brown rice recipe step 3.

6. Preheat oven to 200 degrees.

7. Follow mussels recipe step 2. Prepare herbs and scallions for mussels recipe and herbs for brown rice recipe. Chop pecans for asparagus recipe.

8. Follow brown rice recipe step 4 and mussels recipe steps 3 and 4.

9. While sauce is simmering, follow asparagus recipe step 5 and place serving platter for mussels and serving bowl for rice in oven.

10. Follow brown rice recipe step 5.

11. Follow mussels recipe step 5.

12. Follow asparagus recipe step 6, brown rice recipe step 6, mussels recipe step 6, and serve.

RECIPES

Steamed Mussels

3 pounds mussels
6 cloves garlic
2 tablespoons unsalted butter
1 cup chopped scallions
¼ cup chopped parsley
1 cup chopped artichoke hearts or bottoms
1½ teaspoons chopped fresh tarragon, or
   ½ teaspoon dried
Salt and freshly ground pepper
¾ cup dry white wine

1. With stiff brush, scrub mussels under cold running water. Pull off any beards. Place in large bowl with cold water to cover and set aside until ready to steam. Before steaming, discard any mussels with open shells.

2. Peel garlic and chop finely.

3. In large saucepan, melt butter over medium heat. Add garlic, scallions, parsley, artichoke hearts, tarragon, and salt and pepper to taste and cook until vegetables are tender but not browned, 4 to 5 minutes.

4. Add wine and ¼ cup water, and simmer 5 minutes. Then raise heat to high and bring to a boil.

5. Add mussels, cover pan, and steam until mussels have opened, about 5 minutes. Discard any mussels with unopened shells.

6. Transfer mussels to warm platter and spoon juices over them.

Brown Rice with Roasted Red Pepper

1 cup brown rice
3 tablespoons unsalted butter
Salt

Medium-size red bell pepper
¼ cup chopped parsley
2 tablespoons chopped chives
Freshly ground pepper

1. In medium-size saucepan with tight-fitting cover, combine rice, 2½ cups water, 1 tablespoon of the butter, and ½ teaspoon salt. Bring to a vigorous boil over high heat.

2. Reduce heat until water is just simmering. Cover and continue to simmer 45 minutes. Do not remove lid.

3. Wash red pepper and pat dry with paper towel. Roast pepper by holding with long 2-pronged fork over gas burner flame, or roast in broiler, turning until skin is brown and blistered. Immediately put pepper in brown paper bag, roll up end, and allow pepper to steam about 5 minutes. Remove pepper from bag and allow to cool.

4. When pepper is cool enough to handle, gently remove charred skin. Core, halve, and seed. Chop enough pepper to measure ½ cup and set aside.

5. When rice is cooked, remove from heat and set aside, covered.

6. Add remaining 2 tablespoons butter, red pepper, parsley, chives, and salt and pepper to taste to the cooked rice and toss with fork to combine. Turn rice into warm bowl and serve.

Asparagus Vinaigrette with Pecans

1 pound asparagus
¼ cup plus 2 tablespoons virgin olive oil
2 tablespoons red wine vinegar
Dash of dry mustard
Pinch of freshly ground pepper
Pinch of sugar
¼ cup coarsely chopped pecans

1. Wash asparagus spears and break off tough ends. Peel stalks, if desired.

2. In medium-size skillet, bring approximately 2 cups water to a boil over medium-high heat.

3. Carefully arrange asparagus in skillet, making sure that spears lie flat—water should just cover them. Return water to a boil and cook asparagus, covered, over medium-high heat, until *al dente*, about 3 minutes.

4. Transfer to colander, refresh under cold running water, and drain thoroughly. Transfer to plate, cover with plastic wrap, and refrigerate until cool.

5. In small bowl, combine olive oil, vinegar, mustard, pepper, and sugar, and mix with fork.

6. Transfer asparagus to serving platter, pour vinaigrette over them, and top with pecans.

LEFTOVER SUGGESTIONS

Use leftover roasted red pepper strips as a garnish for salads or omelets. Or chop the pepper into tiny dice and stir into plain yogurt for an hors d'oeuvre dip. For more leftovers, roast 2 peppers and refrigerate leftovers in 4 parts olive oil and 1 part vinegar to cover in a closed container.

Bourbon-Basted Salmon
Bulgur Pilaf
Spinach and Kiwi Salad

Broiled salmon fillets make a festive meal with herbed bulgur pilaf and a salad tossed with honey dressing.

The salmon fillets or steaks are broiled with a bourbon-flavored basting mixture. The accompanying pilaf consists of seasoned bulgur—whole wheat kernels that have been steamed, dried and crushed. This Middle Eastern grain staple has a full, nutty taste and cooks as quickly as white rice. For best results, purchase plain, unseasoned bulgur from your supermarket or health food store.

Kiwi, a fuzzy, brown-skinned fruit, has lime-green flesh, tiny edible black seeds, and a sweet-tart flavor. To ripen hard kiwi, leave in a closed brown paper bag with an apple or a banana at room temperature.

WHAT TO DRINK

A medium-bodied wine would be compatible here: either a dry California Chenin Blanc or a dry French Vouvray.

SHOPPING LIST AND STAPLES

Four ¾- to 1-inch-thick salmon fillets or steaks
  (each about 8 ounces)
Small bunch spinach
Small bunch mustard greens or any tart, crisp green
Small head red-leaf lettuce

101

Medium-size onion
Small red onion
1 clove garlic
Small bunch parsley
Small bunch fresh thyme, or ½ teaspoon dried
Large ripe kiwi
1 lemon
2 tablespoons unsalted butter
2 cups chicken stock, preferably homemade (see page 13), or canned
½ cup virgin olive oil
3 tablespoons safflower oil
3 tablespoons soy sauce
2 tablespoons honey, approximately
1 cup bulgur
Salt and freshly ground white pepper
½ cup bourbon

UTENSILS

Medium-size skillet with cover
Small saucepan
13 x 9 x 2-inch baking pan
Small plate
2 small bowls
Salad bowl
Salad spinner (optional)
Measuring cups and spoons
Chef's knife
Paring knife
Wooden spoon
Metal spatula
Small whisk
Basting brush

START-TO-FINISH STEPS

1. Chop parsley and onion for bulgur recipe, and peel and slice garlic for salad dressing.
2. Follow salad recipe step 1.
3. Follow salmon recipe steps 1 through 4.
4. Follow bulgur recipe steps 1 and 2, and salmon recipe step 5.
5. Follow salad recipe steps 2 through 5.
6. Follow salmon recipe step 6.
7. Follow salad recipe step 6, bulgur recipe step 3, salmon recipe step 7, and serve.

RECIPES

Bourbon-Basted Salmon

½ cup bourbon
½ cup virgin olive oil
3 tablespoons soy sauce
Four ¾- to 1-inch thick salmon fillets or steaks (each about 8 ounces)

1. Preheat oven to 450 degrees.

2. In small bowl, combine bourbon, olive oil, and soy sauce, and whisk until blended.
3. Wipe salmon with damp paper towels.
4. Line baking pan with aluminum foil and place salmon skin side down.
5. Brush salmon with basting mixture and bake, uncovered, basting 2 or 3 times, until fish flakes easily when tested with tip of small knife, 15 to 20 minutes.
6. In small saucepan, bring remaining basting mixture to a boil over medium-high heat. Reduce heat and simmer 3 to 4 minutes.
7. With spatula, transfer salmon fillets to dinner plates and serve basting mixture on the side.

Bulgur Pilaf

2 tablespoons unsalted butter
1 cup bulgur
½ cup chopped onion
2 cups chicken stock
1½ teaspoons minced fresh thyme, or ½ teaspoon dried, crumbled
Salt and freshly ground white pepper
3 tablespoons chopped parsley

1. In medium-size skillet, melt butter over medium heat. Add bulgur and onion, and sauté 5 to 7 minutes, or until bulgur is golden and onion is tender .
2. Add stock, thyme, and salt and pepper to taste. Cover skillet and bring to a boil. Reduce heat and simmer 15 minutes. Keep covered until ready to serve.
3. Just before serving, add parsley and toss with fork.

Spinach and Kiwi Salad

3 cups spinach
1 cup mustard greens or any tart crisp green
2 cups red-leaf lettuce
Large ripe kiwi
Small red onion
3 tablespoons safflower oil
2 tablespoons honey, approximately
Juice of 1 lemon
1 clove garlic, peeled and cut into slivers
Salt and freshly ground white pepper

1. Remove stems from spinach and mustard greens and discard. Wash spinach, greens, and lettuce, and dry in salad spinner or pat dry with paper towels. Tear into bite-size pieces. Place greens in salad bowl, cover with plastic wrap, and refrigerate.
2. Peel and slice kiwi.
3. Peel onion and cut into thin slices.
4. Place kiwi and onion slices on small plate, cover with plastic wrap, and refrigerate.
5. In small bowl, combine remaining ingredients and whisk until blended. Set aside until ready to serve salad. Remove garlic just before tossing greens with dressing.
6. Toss greens with dressing, divide among individual salad bowls, and garnish with kiwi and red onion.

Acknowledgments

Special thanks are due to Gene Cope, International Trade Specialist, National Marine Fisheries Service, Washington, D.C., for his assistance in the preparation of this volume.

The Editors would also like to thank the following for their courtesy in lending items for photography: *Cover:* flatware—Buccellati Silversmiths. *Pages 18–19:* china, ramekins—Broadway Panhandler; napkins—The Basket Handler; underplates—Phillip Meuller, courtesy of Wolfman, Gold & Good Co. *Page 22:* plate—Janis Schneider, courtesy of Downtown Potters' Hall; linens—Laura Ashley. *Page 25:* flatware—Wallace Silversmiths; platters—Richard Ginori Corp.; napkin—Leacock & Company; cloth—Conrans. *Pages 28–29:* flatware—Wallace Silversmiths; platters, cloth—St. Remy. *Pages 32–33:* bowl—Claudia Shwide, courtesy of Creative Resources; cloth—China Seas, Inc. *Page 35:* flatware—Wallace Silversmiths; crystal, china—Wedgwood; napkin—Leacock & Company. *Pages 38–39:* flatware, linens, china—Ludwig Beck of Munich. *Page 42:* flatware, glass—Barney's Chelsea Passage; china—Fitz & Floyd; tiles—Amaru's Tile Selections.

Page 45: servers—Robert D. Murray & Associates; napkins—Ad Hoc Softwares; platters, tureen—Kuttner Antiques. *Pages 48–49:* plate, linens—Pierre Deux. *Page 52:* dishes—Feu Follet. *Page 55:* flatware—Ad Hoc Housewares; tureen, platters—Hutschenreuther; napkins—Leacock & Company; cloth—Conrans. *Pages 58–59:* flatware—Wallace Silversmiths; plate—Beth Forer. *Page 62:* napkin—Leacock & Company; cloth—Conrans; plate—Dorothy Hafner. *Page 66:* flatware—Buccellati Silversmiths; cloth—Handloom Batik Importers; plates—The Museum Store of the Museum of Modern Art. *Pages 68–69:* flatware—The Lauffer Company; china, linens—Pierre Deux. *Page 72:* platter—Buffalo China, Inc.; linens—Ad Hoc Softwares. *Pages 74–75:* flatware—The Lauffer Company; china—Dan Bleier, courtesy of Creative Resources; napkin—Conrans; countertop—Formica® Brand Laminate by Formica Corp. *Pages 78–79:* servers—Dean & DeLuca; platters—Arabia; quilt—Primitive Artisans; napkin—Leacock & Company. *Pages 82–83:* flatware—Wallace Silversmiths; napkins—Leacock & Company; underplates, plates—

Patino/Wolf Associates, Inc. *Page 84:* paper—Four Hands Bindery; plates—Dan Bleier, courtesy of Creative Resources. *Pages 86–87:* flatware—Wallace Silversmiths; napkins—Leacock & Company; plates—Rorstrand; glasses—Kosta Boda; handpainted cloth—Peter Fasano. *Page 90:* flatware—The Lauffer Company; china—Hornsea. *Page 92:* flatware—The Lauffer Company; dinner plate, cloths—New Country Gear. *Pages 94–95:* chopsticks—Mitsukoshi Gallery; obi, dishes—Diane Love, Inc. *Pages 98–99:* flatware—Wallace Silversmiths; plate, bowl—Ad Hoc Housewares; platter—Barney's Chelsea Passage; tiles—Amaru's Tile Selections. *Page 101:* flatware—Wallace Silversmiths; china—Diane Love, Inc.; napkin—Leacock & Company. *Kitchen equipment courtesy of:* White-Westinghouse, Commercial Aluminum Cookware Co., Robot-Coupe, Caloric, Hobart Corp. Microwave oven compliments of Litton Microwave Cooking Products.

Illustrations by Ray Skibinski
Production by Giga Communications

Index

Almonds, baked rice with, 39–41
anchovies, 12
apple cider vinegar, 17
Araldo, Josephine, 4
  menus of, 48–57
artichokes, Jerusalem, and
    Brussels sprouts salad, 65
asparagus
  with lemon glaze, 28–31
  vinaigrette with pecans, 95,
    98–100
avocado
  Bibb lettuce, and tomato salad,
    90–91
  and grapefruit salad, with
    walnut oil dressing, 39–41
  and potato soup, 48, 52–53

Baking, 12, 14
balsamic vinegar, 17
barbecuing, 12
basil toasts, 28, 32–34
Bibb lettuce, avocado, and tomato
    salad, 90–91
blackberry and cantaloupe
    compote, 81
blanching, 15
Bogdonoff, Stacy, 4
  menus of, 28–37

bourbon-basted salmon, 95,
    101–102
braising, 12, 14
bread crumbs, 17
breads
  basil toasts, 28, 32–34
  garlic, 71
Breton coffee cream, 57
broiling, 12, 14
brook trout, fillets of, with
    mushroom sauce, 86, 92–93
brown rice, 17
  with roasted red pepper, 95,
    98–100
  with walnuts, 19, 22–24
Brussels sprouts and cucumbers,
    48, 55–57
  and Jerusalem artichokes
    salad, 65
bulgur pilaf, 95, 101–102
butter, 17
  clarified, 12–13
  cookies, coconut, 44
  fennel sauce, 76
  herb, 37, 88–89
  spiced citrus, 21
butterfly fillets, 9 *illus.*

Cabbage, sautéed new, 19–21

cake, Carlo's chocolate
    earthquake, 47
cantaloupe and blackberry
    compote, 81
capers, 16
Carlo's chocolate earthquake
    cake, 47
carrots and grapes, sautéed,
    48–51
celery, endive and watercress,
    lemon-braised, 25–27
chard in butter and garlic, 39,
    45–47
cheese, 17
  chèvre Florentine, 68–71
  sweet, with crackers and
    assorted fruit, 97
chèvre Florentine, 68–71
chicken liver mousse, 86, 92–93
chicken stock, 13
chili sauce, 83
chocolate
  earthquake cake, Carlo's, 47
  soufflé, 54
chowder
  fish, Mediterranean, 28, 32–34
  seafood curry, 86, 90–91
  see also stew
clam juice, 16

cake, Carlo's chocolate
clams
  characteristics of, 11
  form of, in markets, 9
  freshness of, 9
  preparation of, 10
  seafood soup Provençale, 68–71
  in sesame-ginger sauce, 59,
    66–67
cleaning fish, 9–10 *illus.*
Cliborne, Bruce, 5
  menus of, 59–67
coconut
  butter cookies, 44
  cream, mussels and shrimp in,
    59, 62–64
cod
  characteristics of, 11
  substitutes for, 11
  see also fish
coffee cream, Breton, 57
cookies, coconut butter, 44
cooking equipment, 15
cooking safety, 8
cooking techniques, 12–14
corn oil, 16
cornstarch, 16
crab
  characteristics of, 11
  freshness of, 8

and hazelnut stuffing, haddock
with, 25–27
see also shellfish
Creole fish and oyster stew, 39–41
cucumber, seeding, 57 *illus.*
cucumbers and Brussels sprouts,
48, 55–57
cumin-orange sauce, 81
curry chowder, seafood, 86, 90–91
cusk, 11

Deep frying, 12
desserts
Breton coffee cream, 57
cantaloupe and blackberry
compote, 81
Carlo's chocolate earthquake
cake, 47
chocolate soufflé, 54
coconut butter cookies, 44
strawberries and white wine
sabayon, 71
sweet cheese with crackers and
assorted fruit, 97
Dover sole, 11
drawn fish, 9
dressed fish, 9 *illus.*
dressing fish, 9–10 *illus.*

Eggs, 17
endive
with celery and watercress,
lemon-braised, 25–27
and watercress salad with
warm olive oil dressing, 28,
32–34

Fat
content of fish, 12
cooking safely with, 8
for sautéing, 12–13
fennel
braised, 77
butter sauce, 76
and fresh tomato soup, 39,
45–47
fettuccine with garlic and oil, 59,
66–67
filleting, 10
fillets, 9 *illus.*
fish
baked in parchment with red
peppers, 39, 42–44
cleaning, 9–10
cooking techniques, 12–14
dressing, 10
dumplings (*quenelles*) with
shallot sauce, 48–51
fat content of, 12
freshness of, 8
forms of, in markets, 9
frozen, 14
nutritional benefits of, 7
and oyster stew, Creole, 39–41
scaling, 9
seafood soup Provençale, 68–71
selection of, 8–9
skinning, 10
stew, Mediterranean, 28, 32–34
storage of, 12, 14

substitutions of, for recipes, 11
see also names of fish
fish stock, 13
flambéing, 14
flatfish
characteristics of, 11
dressing, 10 *illus.*
see also names of flatfish
flounder
characteristics of, 11
fat content of, 12
substitutes for, 11
see also fish
French-style dishes
chèvre Florentine, 68–71
garden salad with mustard
vinaigrette, 68, 74–77
julienned vegetables, 72–73
quenelles with shallot sauce,
48–51
rainbow trout, 68, 72–73
saffron rice mold, 68, 72–73
sautéed scallops with white
wine sauce, 59–61
sea bass with fennel-butter
sauce, 68, 74–76
seafood soup Provençale, 68–71
warm potato salad, 74–77
frozen fish, 14
fruit
assorted, with sweet cheese
and crackers, 97
dried, 16
see also names of fruits
frying, 12–13, 14

Garden salad with mustard
vinaigrette, 68, 74–77
garlic, 16
garlic bread, 71
gazpacho, 89
ginger, fresh, 17
and sesame sauce, 67
goosefish
characteristics of, 11
seafood soup Provençale, 70–71
substitute for, 11
grapefruit and avocado salad,
with walnut oil dressing,
39–41
grapes and carrots, sautéed,
48–51
green rice, 82–83
green sauce, 31

Haddock
characteristics of, 11
with crab meat and hazelnut
stuffing, 25–27
see also fish
halibut
characteristics of, 11
substitutes for, 11
see also fish
hazelnut and crab meat stuffing,
haddock with, 25–27
herb butter, 37, 88–89
herbs, 16

Italian plum tomatoes, 17

Jalapeño pepper, 40
Jerusalem artichokes and
Brussels sprouts salad, 65,
65 *illus.*
jícama
hors d'oeuvres, 97
in salads, 97
and snow peas, 95–97
as substitute for water
chestnuts, 97
Johnson, Linda, 5
menus of, 95–102

King mackerel, 11
kiwi and spinach salad, 95,
101–102
kohlrabi, stuffed, 62–65, 65 *illus.*

Land, Leslie, 4
menus of, 19–27
lean fish, 12
leeks, with new potatoes, braised
in broth, 28, 35–37
lemon(s), 17
sauce, 57
lima bean soup, 48, 55–56
lime-parsley sauce, 23–24
lobster
characteristics of, 11
fat content of, 12
freshness of, 8
preparation of, 11
steamed, with four sauces,
19–21

Mackerel
characteristics of, 11
fat content of, 12
Mediterranean fish stew, 28,
32–34
substitutes for, 11
see also fish
mako shark, 11
Mediterranean fish stew, 28,
32–34
Mexican-style dishes
baked red snapper with chili
sauce, 79, 82–83
broiled tuna with orange-cumin
sauce, 79–81
green rice, 82–83
oyster seviche, 79, 82–83
sauté of squash, onion, and
peppers, 79–81
spicy squid salad, 79–81
Miller, Mark, 5
menus of, 79–85
mullet, 11
mushroom(s), 61 *illus.*
sauce, 93
wild, salad, with basil and mint,
59–61
mussels
characteristics of, 11
form of, in markets, 9
freshness of, 9
preparation of, 10–11
seafood soup Provençale, 68–71
and shrimp in coconut cream
with mint, 59, 62–64

steamed, 95, 98–100
see also shellfish
mustard vinaigrette, 77

Neuman, Paul, 4
menus of, 28–37
new potatoes, 17
with basil, 39, 45–47
braised in broth with leeks, 28,
35–37

Oils, 16
olive oil
characteristics of, 17
sautéing with, 13
onions, 16–17
with squash and peppers, sauté
of, 79–81
orange-cumin sauce, 81
Oriental-style dishes
clams in sesame-ginger sauce,
59, 66–67
mixed vegetables, 59, 66–67
orzo with poppy seeds, 95–97
oysters
characteristics of, 11
and fish stew, Creole, 39–41
form of, in markets, 9
freshness of, 9
poached, with saffron-cream
sauce, 79, 84–85
preparation of, 11
seviche, 79, 82–83

Pan-dressed fish, 9 *illus.*
pan frying, 12
pantry, 16–17
parboiling, 14
parsley, 17
pasta
fettuccine with garlic and oil,
59, 66–67
orzo with poppy seeds, 95–97
pears in red wine, spiced, 77
peas, *see* snow peas
pecans, asparagus vinaigrette
with, 95, 98–100
peppers
jalapeño, 40
red, *see* red bell peppers
pilaf
bulgur, 95, 101–102
rice, with scallions, 28–31
poaching, 12, 14
polenta with butter and cheese,
39, 42–44
potato(es), 17
and avocado soup, 48, 52–53
new, with basil, 39, 45–47
new, braised in broth with
leeks, 28, 35–37
with onions and cheese, 48–51
oven-fried, 19–21
riced, with parsley, 86–89,
89 *illus.*
salad, warm, 74–77
prawns
characteristics of, 11
with green peppercorns, 95–97
preparation of, 11

Quenelles with shallot sauce, 48–51

Rainbow trout, 68, 72–73
red bell pepper(s)
    cooked, storage of, 100
    fish baked in parchment with, 39, 42–44
    as garnish, 100
    roasted, with brown rice, 95, 98–100
    with squash and onions, sauté of, 79–81
    and yogurt hors d'oeuvres, 100
red snapper
    baked, with chili sauce, 79, 82–83
    characteristics of, 11
    fat content of, 12
    substitutes for, 11
    see also fish
red wine, spiced pears in, 77
rice, 17
    with almonds, baked, 39–41
    brown, with roasted red pepper, 95, 98–100
    green, 82–83
    mold, saffron, 68, 72–73
    pilaf with scallions, 28–31
    spicy, 86, 92–93
    with walnuts, 19, 22–24
round fish, dressing, 10 *illus.*

Sabayon, white wine, with strawberries, 71
saffron
    cream sauce, 85
    rice mold, 68, 72–73
salad
    asparagus vinaigrette with pecans, 95, 98–100
    avocado and grapefruit, with walnut oil dressing, 39–41
    Bibb lettuce, avocado, and tomato, 90–91
    Jerusalem artichokes and Brussels sprouts, 65
    marinated, 39, 42–44
    rice and shark steak, 24
    spinach and kiwi, 95, 101–102
    squid, spicy, 79–81
    warm potato, 74–77
    watercress and endive with warm olive oil dressing, 28, 32–34
    wild mushrooms with basil and mint, 59–61
salmon
    à la tartare, 79, 84–85
    bourbon-basted, 95, 101–102
    characteristics of, 11
    fat content of, 12
    poached, wtih green sauce, 28–31
    see also fish
Sanderson, Kathleen Kenny, 5
    menus of, 68–77
sauces
    chili, 83
    fennel-butter, 76

green, 31
herb butter, 37, 88–89
lemon, 57
lime-parsley, 23–24
mushroom, 93
orange-cumin, 81
saffron cream, 85
sesame-ginger, 67
shallot, 51
sour cream, 21
spiced citrus butter, 21
tempura, 21
wasabi, 21
white wine, 53–54, 61
sautéing, 12–13
sauté pan, 12, 15
scaling, 9 *illus.*
scallops
    characteristics of, 11
    fat content of, 12
    form of, in markets, 9
    sautéed, with white wine sauce, 59–61
scrod, 11
sea bass
    characteristics of, 11
    fat content of, 12
    with fennel-butter sauce, 68, 74–76
    substitutes for, 11
    see also fish
seafood, *see* fish; shellfish; names of fish and shellfish
sesame
    ginger sauce, 67
    oil, 16
seviche, oyster, 79, 82–83
shallot(s), 17
    sauce, 51
    with spinach, sautéed, 28, 35–37
shark
    broiled steaks with lime-parsley sauce, 19, 22–24
    characteristics of, 11
    freshness of, 8
shellfish
    classification of, 7
    fat content of, 12
    forms of, in markets, 9
    freshness of, 8–9
    frozen, 14
    nutritional benefits of, 7
    preparation of, 10–12
    seafood soup Provençale, 68–71
    selection of, 8–9
    storage of, 12, 14
    type of, for recipes, 11
    see also names of shellfish
sherry vinegar, 17
shrimp
    characteristics of, 11
    fat content of, 12
    freshness of, 8
    and mussels in coconut cream with mint, 59, 62–64
    prawns with green peppercorns, 95–97
    preparation of, 11
    seafood soup Provençale, 68–71

silver hake, *see* whiting
skinning fish, 10
snow peas
    and jícama, 95–97
    sautéed with water chestnuts, 86–89, 89 *illus.*
sole
    characteristics of, 11
    fat content of, 12
    fillets of, in herb butter, 86–89
    fillets of, in wine sauce, 48, 52–54
soufflé, chocolate, 54
soup
    avocado and potato, 48, 52–53
    fresh tomato and fennel, 39, 45–47
    gazpacho, 89
    lima bean, 48, 55–56
    seafood curry chowder, 86, 90–91
    seafood Provençale, 68–71
sour cream sauce, 21
spices, 16
spinach
    and kiwi salad, 95, 101–102
    sauté, spicy, 59–61
    with shallots, sautéed, 28, 35–37
squash with onions and peppers, sauté of, 79–81
squid
    characteristics of, 11
    form of, in markets, 9
    freshness of, 9
    preparation of, 11–12
    salad, spicy, 79–81
steaks, fish, 9 *illus.*
steaming, 12, 13
stew
    Creole fish and oyster, 39–41
    seafood soup Provençale, 68–71
sticks, fish, 9 *illus.*
stir frying, 12, 14
stock, 17
    chicken, 13
    fish, 13
storage of seafood, 12, 14
strawberries and white wine sabayon, 71
Swiss chard in butter and garlic, 39, 45–47
swordfish
    broiled, with herb butter, 28, 35–37
    characteristics of, 11
    substitute for, 11
    see also fish

Tempura sauce, 21
thawing frozen fish, 14
Thorstensson, Elisabeth, 5
    menus of, 86–93
toasts, basil, 28, 32–34
tomatoes, 17
    Bibb lettuce, and avocado salad, 90–91
    fresh, and fennel soup, 39, 45–47

trout
    baked in coarse salt, 39, 45–47
    brook, fillets of, with mushroom sauce, 86, 92–93
    characteristics of, 11
    rainbow, 68, 72–73
    see also fish
tuna
    broiled, with orange-cumin sauce, 79–81
    characteristics of, 11
    fat content of, 12
    substitutes for, 11
    see also fish

Unterman, Patricia, 4
    menus of, 39–47

Vegetable oil, 16
vegetables
    broiled, 19, 22–24
    gazpacho, 89
    julienned, 72–73
    mixed, Oriental-style, 59, 66–67
    see also names of vegetables
vinaigrette
    asparagus, with pecans, 95, 98–100
    mustard, 77
vinegars, 17

Walnut oil, 16
    dressing, 39–41
wasabi sauce, 21
water chestnuts, 17
    with sautéed snow peas, 86–89
    substitute for, 97
watercress and endive salad with warm olive oil dressing, 28, 32–34
white wine
    sabayon, with strawberries, 71
    sauce, 53–54, 61
whiting
    characteristics of, 11
    with lemon sauce, 48, 55–57
    see also fish
whole fish, 9 *illus.*
wines, 17
    see also red wine; white wine

Zucchini Merveille, 48, 52–54

Time-Life Books Inc. offers a wide range of fine recordings, including a Big Band series. For subscription information, call 1-800-621-7026, or write TIME-LIFE MUSIC, Time & Life Building, Chicago, Illinois 60611.